General editor: Graham Handley MA PhD

Brodie's Notes on William Shakespeare's
Coriolanus

Kevin Dowling MA
Formerly Director of Studies and Head of English, Bembridge School

Pan Books London, Sydney and Auckland

First published 1987 by Pan Books Ltd,
Cavaye Place, London SW10 9PG
9 8 7 6 5 4 3 2
© Pan Books Ltd 1987
ISBN 0 330 50224 7
Photoset by Parker Typesetting Service, Leicester
Made and printed in Great Britain by
Richard Clay Ltd, Bungay, Suffolk

Other titles by Kevin Dowling in the Brodie's Notes series:
Persuasion Jane Austen
The War of the Worlds H. G. Wells

Contents

Line references in these Notes are to the *Arden Shakespeare*: *Coriolanus*, but as references are also given to particular scenes, the Notes may be used with any edition of the play.

Preface

This student revision aid is based on the principle that in any close examination of Shakespeare's plays 'the text's the thing'. Seeing a performance, or listening to a tape or record of a performance, is essential and is in itself a valuable and stimulating experience in understanding and appreciation. However, a real evaluation of Shakespeare's greatness, of his universality and of the nature of his literary and dramatic art, can only be achieved by constant application to the texts of the plays themselves. These revised editions of Brodie's Notes are intended to supplement that process through detailed critical commentary.

The first aim of each book is to fix the whole play in the reader's mind by providing a concise summary of the plot, relating it back, where appropriate, to its source or sources. Subsequently the book provides a summary of each scene, followed by *critical comments*. These may convey its importance in the dramatic structure of the play, creation of atmosphere, indication of character development, significance of figurative language etc., and they will also explain or paraphrase difficult words or phrases and identify meaningful references. At the end of each act revision questions are set to test the student's specific and broad understanding and appreciation of the play.

An extended critical commentary follows this scene by scene analysis. This embraces such major elements as characterization, imagery, the use of blank verse and prose, soliloquies and other aspects of the play which the editor considers need close attention. The paramount aim is to send the reader back to the text. The book concludes with a series of revision questions which require a detailed knowledge of the play; the first of these has notes by the editor of what *might* be included in a written answer. The intention is to stimulate and to guide; the whole emphasis of this commentary is to encourage the student's *involvement* in the play, to develop disciplined critical responses and thus promote personal enrichment through the imaginative experience of our greatest writer.

Graham Handley

Shakespeare and the Elizabethan Playhouse

William Shakespeare was born in Stratford-upon-Avon in 1564, and there are reasons to suppose that he came from a relatively prosperous family. He was probably educated at Stratford Grammar School and, at the age of eighteen, married Anne Hathaway, who was twenty-six. They had three children, a girl born shortly after their marriage, followed by twins in 1585 (the boy died in 1596). It seems likely that Shakespeare left for London shortly after a company of travelling players had visited Stratford in 1585, for by 1592 – according to the jealous testimony of one of his fellow-writers, Robert Greene – he was certainly making his way both as actor and dramatist. The theatres were closed because of the plague in 1593; when they reopened Shakespeare worked with the Lord Chamberlain's men, later the King's men, and became a shareholder in each of the two theatres with which he was most closely associated, the Globe and the Blackfriars. He later purchased New Place, a considerable property in his home town of Stratford, to which he retired in 1611; there he entertained his great contemporary Ben Jonson (1572–1637) and the poet Michael Drayton (1563–1631). An astute businessman, Shakespeare lived comfortably in the town until his death in 1616.

This is a very brief outline of the life of our greatest writer, for little more can be said of him with certainty, though the plays – and poems – are living witness to the wisdom, humanity and many-faceted nature of the man. He was both popular and successful as a dramatist, perhaps less so as an actor. He probably began work as a dramatist in the late 1580s, by collaborating with other playwrights and adapting old plays, and by 1598 Francis Meres was paying tribute to his excellence in both comedy and tragedy. His first original play was probably *Love's Labour's Lost* (1590) and while the theatres were closed during the plague he wrote his narrative poems *Venus and Adonis* (1593) and *The Rape of Lucrece* (1594). The sonnets were almost certainly written in the 1590s though not published until 1609; the first 126 are addressed to a young man who was his friend and patron, while the rest are concerned with the 'dark lady'.

The dating of Shakespeare's plays has exercised scholars ever since the publication of the First Folio (1623), which listed them as comedies, histories and tragedies. It seems more important to look at them chronologically as far as possible, in order to trace Shakespeare's considerable development as a dramatist. The first period, say to the middle of the 1590s, included such plays as *Love's Labour's Lost*, *The Comedy of Errors*, *Richard III*, *The Taming of the Shrew*, *Romeo and Juliet* and *Richard II*. These early plays embrace the categories listed in the First Folio, so that Shakespeare the craftsman is evident in his capacity for variety of subject and treatment. The next phase includes *A Midsummer Night's Dream*, *The Merchant of Venice*, *Henry IV Parts 1 and 2*, *Henry V* and *Much Ado About Nothing*, as well as *Julius Caesar*, *As You Like It* and *Twelfth Night*. These are followed, in the early years of the century, by his great tragic period: *Hamlet*, *Othello*, *King Lear* and *Macbeth*, with *Antony and Cleopatra* and *Coriolanus* belonging to 1607–09. The final phase embraces the romances (1610–13), *Cymbeline*, *The Tempest* and *The Winter's Tale* and the historical play *Henry VIII*.

Each of these revision aids will place the individual text under examination in the chronology of the remarkable dramatic output that spanned twenty years from the early 1590s to about 1613. The practical theatre for which Shakespeare wrote and acted derived from the inn courtyards in which performances had taken place, the few playhouses in his day being modelled on their structure. They were circular or hexagonal in shape, allowing the balconies and boxes around the walls full view of the stage. This large stage, which had no scenery, jutted out into the pit, the most extensive part of the theatre, where the poorer people – the 'groundlings' – stood. There was no roof (though the Blackfriars, used from 1608 onwards, was an indoor theatre) and thus bad weather meant no performance. Certain plays were acted at court, and these private performances normally marked some special occasion. Costumes, often rich ones, were used, and music was a common feature, with musicians on or under the stage; this sometimes had additional features, for example a trapdoor to facilitate the entry of a ghost. Women were barred by law from appearing on stage, and all female parts were played by boy actors; this undoubtedly explains the many instances in Shakespeare where a woman has to conceal her identity by disguising

herself as a man, e.g. Rosalind in *As You Like It*, Viola in *Twelfth Night*.

Shakespeare and his contemporaries often adapted their plays from sources in history and literature, extending an incident or a myth or creating a dramatic narrative from known facts. They were always aware of their own audiences, and frequently included topical references, sometimes of a satirical flavour, which would appeal to – and be understood by – the groundlings as well as their wealthier patrons who occupied the boxes. Shakespeare obviously learned much from his fellow dramatists and actors, being on good terms with many of them. Ben Jonson paid generous tribute to him in the lines prefaced to the First Folio of Shakespeare's plays:

Thou art a monument without a tomb,
And art alive still, while thy book doth live
And we have wits to read, and praise to give.

Among his contemporaries were Thomas Kyd (1558–94) and Christopher Marlowe (1564–93). Kyd wrote *The Spanish Tragedy*, the revenge motif here foreshadowing the much more sophisticated treatment evident in *Hamlet*, while Marlowe evolved the 'mighty line' of blank verse, a combination of natural speech and elevated poetry. The quality and variety of Shakespeare's blank verse owes something to the innovatory brilliance of Marlowe but carries the stamp of individuality, richness of association, technical virtuosity and, above all, the genius of imaginative power.

The texts of Shakespeare's plays are still rich sources for scholars, and the editors of these revision aids have used the Arden editions of Shakespeare, which are regarded as preeminent for their scholarly approach. They are strongly recommended for advanced students, but other editions, like the New Penguin Shakespeare, the New Swan, the Signet are all good annotated editions currently available. A reading list of selected reliable works on the play being studied is provided at the end of each commentary and students are advised to turn to these as their interest in the play deepens.

Literary terms used in these notes

irony A deeper meaning which is derived from the opposite of what is stated literally: consider the effect of the word 'noble' in I,1, 246; I,3,67.

tragic irony A situation or a statement that has a significance unperceived at the time, and often where fate seems later to mock the human condition: examine Coriolanus's words in I,1,181 & 219,230,238 for example.

dramatic irony The character is unaware of the truth or untruth of his words, but the audience and possibly the other characters on stage are: notable examples are IV,6,8; V,4,6; V,4,11 when I,3,61 is recalled; all V,3.

hubris Blind, arrogant pride such as invites disaster.

iambic pentameter The line of verse is made up of five feet (pentameter), each consisting of two syllables, the first of which is unstressed and the second stressed (iambs):
'Wĭth év|eřy mín|ŭte vóu|dŏ chánge|ă mínd,
Aňd cáll|hĭm nó|blĕ tȟat|wăs nów|yoŭr háte.'

caesura An emphatic pause required by the flow of the sentence, even when no punctuation is given.
'And call him noble·that was now your hate,
Him vile·that was your garland.'

elision The omission of a vowel or a syllable, making the verse more fluid: 'I'th'midst o'th'body'.

syntactical inversion The reversal of common prose order, thus varying emphasis to give rhetorical force: 'That only like a gulf it did remain'.

rhetoric The art of using speech to persuade others.

enjambement The running on of lines to vary pace, frequently to gather rhetorical momentum: '. . . you shall find/No public benefit which you receive/But it proceeds or comes from them to you.'

catharsis A term used by Aristotle in *Poetics*. A therapeutic purification by means of the purgation of the emotions of pity and fear that are aroused by tragedy.

metaphor A figure of speech by which a thing is spoken of as being that which it only resembles; a means of implying comparison without using 'like' or 'as': 'He's a very dog to the commonalty.'

imagery Mental pictures or sense-impressions conveyed by the expression of ideas or entities in terms of others: 'The kingly crown'd head, the vigilant eye,/The counsellor heart, the arm our soldier,/ . . .Should by the cormorant belly be restrain'd/Who is the sink o'th'body'.

Plot, source and treatment

Plot

The play is set in the early years of the Roman Republic, after the defeat of Tarquinus Superbus, the last king of Rome, about the year 496 BC. Coriolanus is the great warrior who leads the Roman forces to victory over the Volscian enemy. He has no political ambition, but is persuaded by his patrician (of noble birth) friends and his family, notably his mother, to stand for election as consul, one of the leaders of the Republic. Respected by the plebeians (citizens, working-people of Rome) for his services to the State, but disliked for his haughty bearing, Coriolanus fails in his bid for consulship because of his undisguised contempt for a political process that seems to him to compromise the dignity and order of the State, by tending to transfer power from responsible authority to the untrustworthy citizens. Tribunes (magistrates) of the people, opposed to Coriolanus's election, and who are appointed by the Senate (the ruling body of the Republic, patrician in composition) to speak for the people at the time of the food shortages when the play opens, easily prevail over the confused public response to the election. Coriolanus is declared a traitor to the Republic because he is known to have spoken critically of the people, to have no respect for democratic tradition, and to have expressed the view that the tribunate should be revoked; by implication, therefore, he is potentially tyrannical.

Expelled from Rome, in revenge he offers his services to the Volsces, in particular to their general, his enemy and rival warrior-hero, Aufidius, lately defeated by Coriolanus. Accepted by the Volsces, he leads their forces against Rome, which is peaceful in his absence, but relatively defenceless without his military genius. The Romans beg Coriolanus to spare the city from destruction. Their initial attempts, first made by Coriolanus's former commanding officer, and second by Menenius, almost a father to Coriolanus, fail to move him. The final plea is made by a family group, led by Volumnia, Coriolanus's mother. Coriolanus is unable to deny natural affections, and cannot go through with his plan.

Coriolanus returns to Corioles with the Volscian general Aufidius. His intention is to justify his decision to make peace, as being in the interest of both the Volsces and the Romans. Aufidius, having felt himself displaced by Coriolanus's reputation and success, plans and perpetrates the assassination of Coriolanus for betrayal of the Volscian cause.

Source

The history of Coriolanus is taken from *The Life of Caius Martius Coriolanus* in Sir Thomas North's translation (1579) of Plutarch's (AD 46–c.120) *Parallel Lives* (a pairing of Greek and Roman heroes, a biographical approach to history). North's translation was made from the French of James Amyot (pub. 1559) who had himself translated Plutarch's Greek. The fable of the belly (I,1,95–153), which is mentioned in Plutarch, is the one section of the play to have other identifiable sources, for example Livy's *Roman History*, translated by Holland (1600), Camden's *Remaines* (1605) and Averell's *A Marvailous Combat of Contrarieties* (1588). North's Elizabethan prose is beautiful in its resonance, dignity and clarity, and Shakespeare's debt to Plutarch can be illustrated by the following extracts:

That a reare and excellent witte untaught, doth bring forth many good and evill things together: like as a fat soile bringeth forth herbes and weedes that lieth unmanured. For this Martius naturall wit and great harte dyd marvelously sturre up his corage, to doe and attempt notable actes. But on the other side for lacke of education, he was so chollericke and impacient, that he would yeld to no living creature: which made him churlishe, uncivill, and altogether unfit for any man's conversation. Yet men marveling much at his constancy, that he was never overcome with pleasure, nor money, and howe he would endure easely all manner of paynes and travailles: thereupon they well liked and commended his stowtnes and temperancie. But for all that, they could not be acquainted with him, as one citizen useth to be with another in the cittie. His behaviour was so unpleasaunt to them, by reason of a certaine insolent and sterne manner he had, which bicause it was to lordly, was disliked. And to saye truely, the greatest benefit that learning bringeth men unto is this: that it teacheth men that be rude and rough of nature, by compasse and rule of reason, to be civill and curteous, and to like better the meane state, than the higher. Nowe in those dayes, valliantnes was honoured in Rome above all other vertues: which they called 'Virtus', by the name of vertue selfe, as including in that generall name, all other speciall vertues besides. So that 'Virtus' in the Latin was asmuche as valliantnes.

. . . Now he being growen to great credit and authoritie in Rome for his valliantnes, it fortuned there grewe sedition in the cittie, because the Senate dyd favour the riche against the people who dyd complaine of the sore oppression of the userers, of whom they borowed money. For those that had litle, were yet spoyled of that litle they had by their creditours, for lack of abilitie to paye the userie: who offered their goodes to be solde, to them that would geve most. And such as had nothing left, their bodies were layed hold of, and they were made bonde men, notwithstanding all the woundes and cuttes they shewed, which they had receyved in many batteles, fighting for defence of their countrie and common wealth.

. . . For Martius alleaged, that the creditours losing their money they had lent, was not the worst thing that was thereby: but that the lenitie that was favored, was a beginning of disobedience, and that the prowde attempt of the communaltie was to abolish lawe, and to bring all to confusion. Therefore he sayed, if the Senate were wise, they should betimes prevent, and quenche this ill favored and worse ment beginning.

. . .Menenius Agrippa knit up his oration in the ende, with a notable tale, in this manner. That on a time all the members of mans bodie, dyd rebell against the bellie, complaining of it, that it only remained in the middest of the bodie, without doing any thing, neither dyd beare any labour to the maintenance of the rest: whereas all other partes and members dyd labour paynefully, and was very carefull to satisfie the appetites and desiers of the bodie. And so the bellie, all this notwith-standing, laughed at their follie, and sayed. It is true, I first receyve all meates that norishe mans bodie: but afterwardes I sent it againe to the norishement of other partes of the same. Even so (quoth he) ô you, my masters and cittizens of Rome: the reason is a like betweene the Senate, and you.

. . .So Junius Brutus, and Sicinius Vellutus, were the first Tribunes of the people that were chosen, who had only bene the causers and procurers of this sedition. Hereupon the cittie being growen againe to good quiet and unitie, the people immediatly went to the warres, shewing that they had a good will to doe better then ever they dyd, and to be very willing to obey the magistrates in that they would command, concerning the warres.

. . . But when the daye of election was come, and that Martius came to the market place with great pompe, accompanied with all the Senate, and the whole Nobilitie of the cittie about him, who sought to make him Consul, with the greatest instance and intreatie they could, or ever attempted for any man or matter: then the love and good will of the common people, turned straight to an hate and envie toward him.

...For Coriolanus's chiefest purpose was, to increase still the malice and dissention between the nobilitie, and the communaltie: and to drawe that on, he was very carefull to keepe the noble mens landes and goods safe from harme and burning, but spoyled all the whole countrie besides, and would suffer no man to take or hurte any thing of the noble mens. This made greater sturre and broyle betweene the nobilitie and people, then was before.

... Nowe was Martius set then in his chayer of state, with all the honours of a generall, and when he had spied the women comming a farre of, he marveled what the matter ment: but afterwardes knowing his wife which came formest, he determined at the first to persist in his obstinate and inflexible rancker. But overcomen in the ende with natur-all affection, and being altogether altered to see them: his harte would not serve him to tarie their comming to his chayer, but comming downe in hast, he went to meet them, and first he kissed his mother, and imbraced her a pretie while, then his wife and little children. And nature so wrought with him, that the teares fell from his eyes, and he could not keepe him selfe from making much of them, but yeelded to the affection of his bloode, as if he had bene violently caried with the furie of a most swift running streame.

Treatment

An appreciation of the differences between Shakespeare's treat-ment of the story and Plutarch's is critical to an understanding of the dramatist's intention. Shakespeare compresses two rebel-lions (usury riots and corn riots) of the common people against the patricians, and two campaigns against Rome by the Volsces into one, and telescopes the setting and timing of events for the purposes of dramatic concentration. Menenius, Plutarch's spokesman for the patricians, is given individual prominence in the play through his relationship with Coriolanus. Volumnia's matriarchal dominance is Shakespeare's invention. Act III, Scene 2, for example, the important prefiguring of Act V, Scene 3, has no counterpart in the source. In Plutarch, Virgilia's silence is the absence of speech; in Shakespeare it is dramatically suggestive. Aufidius, the Volscian enemy referred to in Plutarch only when Coriolanus goes to Antium, is made a personal pro-tagonist and a studied contrast to Coriolanus.

The character of Coriolanus is seen by Plutarch as a combi-nation of good qualities and bad; the deficiencies might well have been remedied by education. Shakespeare presents a man in whom several qualities are inextricably interconnected, a paradox of good and evil. Coriolanus's confrontation with the people is given a complexity it lacks in Plutarch; and the man who enters Corioles alone, who wishes to burn Rome, whose loyalties are tragically divided, and on whom the fate of a city depends, is Shakespeare's invention.

Text and date

Literary allusions and topical references point to the play as having been written between 1605 and 1610. The only text is that of the First Folio (a folio is a book made up of sheets folded once before binding, and having therefore four sides of print on two leaves of paper) of 1623, which was the first collected edition of Shakespeare's plays. This text is divided into Acts but not scenes, which were added by a series of subsequent editors. It should be remembered that, in Elizabethan times, plays were performed as continuous drama on practically a bare stage, therefore the divisions that provide a convenient structure for rehearsal and reading should not be taken as an absolute definition of the construction of the play. The drama is an integral performance, not a series of episodes. No locations are specified in the Folio, but they are usually apparent from the play and have been suggested by editors. The stage directions are particularly interesting as an indication of how the production of the play may have been visualized by Shakespeare.

Scene summaries, critical comment, textual notes and revision questions

Act I Scene 1

The citizens of Rome are about to rebel against their patrician masters, in protest at the price of grain. Menenius Agrippa attempts to pacify them with a metaphorical explanation of the responsibilities of the patricians. Caius Martius (not yet titled Coriolanus) enters and confronts the citizens' anger, while news of war defuses what is left. As preparations are made for the campaign, tribunes – newly appointed in deference to the people's complaints – criticize Martius.

Commentary

The scene is a riot of words – good-humoured debate, invective that seems calculated to inflame rather than subdue, ominous news, and innuendo – and it is a presentation of ideas important in the play: duty and responsibility, civic and personal virtue, the concept of the state as an organism, the nature of political realities.

Martius is immediately the central presence. The scene begins with his being spoken of as 'chief enemy to the people', and ends with the malicious prayer, 'The present wars devour him'. He is reported as much as seen but his appearance in the street does dominate the action, as he silences the mob with withering contempt. To the warrior, the citizens are cowardly, verminous creatures, unstable in their affections and allegiances, crying out against those who protect them against themselves. He derides their presumption, and regrets the compassion of his fellow patricians as being a dangerous indulgence, more likely to foment insurrection than quell it. The manner of Coriolanus's speech offers as great an insight into his character as does his argument. Brave, proud and young, he is in some respects a contrast to all the other characters on the stage. Lately a 'garland', now become 'vile', Martius seems to personify the great engine of the state that Menenius speaks of. Martius is glad of a war that may serve to decimate the rabble, and allow a 'constant' soldier to seek out a noble opposite.

The citizens – armed only with bats and clubs – have a case that is not answered by Menenius or Martius. The revolt is in 'hunger' not in 'revenge', the general urge to proceed against the man who is 'a very dog to the commonalty' is tempered by the second citizen's insistence on Martius's disinterested service of his country, and Menenius is listened to by doubting but reasonable men. 'Almost persuaded' by the fable, their indignation is 'dissolved' by Martius, and they steal away from danger. On stage for most of the scene, their prose is the frame only for the convoluted metaphor of Menenius and the emphatic verse of Martius. The tale of the belly and the members offers to the plebeians a crucial justification of the patricians' plenty: the natural order of mutual dependence requires a 'cupboarding' of the 'viand' so that a 'natural competency' may be diffused through the body. Dramatically, this is a sophisticated deflation of self-righteous anger, punctuated by heckling that challenges both the analogy itself and its intention: 'to fob off our disgrace'.

The tribunes' references to the volatility of the people are a coda to the public clamour of the opening exchanges. The final combination of personal spite and cynical appraisal leaves the audience with the impression of great events keenly observed by opportunists, tacticians preying upon the protagonist. The commanding figure of Martius is already shadowed by those who hate and distrust him more, and with less cause, than does the confused mob.

any further i.e. to th' Capitol. (See line 47.)
verdict i.e. are all agreed?
good Wealthy and worthy.
what authority ... on Those in authority have the surplus grain that would relieve the famine.
but Merely.
guess Think, deduce.
too dear Unworthy of support.
object Sight.
an inventory to particularise their abundance i.e. indicative of the scale of their advantage.
sufferance Suffering.
rakes i.e. as thin as rakes.
but ... proud i.e. an excessive pride is his fee for services rendered.
soft-conscienced i.e. woolly-minded.
to be partly proud To give him reason for pride.
virtue Valour, in the Roman sense.

I need not . . . accusations i.e. there is no lack of offences of which he can be accused.

Capitol i.e. by implication the Senate House.

bats and clubs i.e. weapons, such as London apprentices would use in the sixteenth century.

poor suitors have strong breaths i.e. the poor have bad breath; said in a proverbial manner.

Your knees . . . help You should obey and not oppose them.

transported by calamity Carried away, by the disaster.

helms i.e. those who guide and rule the state.

piercing statutes Harsh laws.

pretty i.e. apt.

to fob off our disgrace To explain away the way we have been treated.

members Limbs. See Romans, 12,4 in the Authorized Version of the Bible.

still cupboarding the viand i.e. always hoarding the food.

like labour Similar work.

appetite and affection common General desires and inclinations.

smile . . . thus i.e. a disdainful smile; possibly Menenius would make some accompanying gesture, with his clothes or even his stomach.

receipt i.e. of food.

fitly i.e. fittingly (ironical?).

muniments Supports.

incorporate i.e. incorporated in one body.

seat i.e. centre.

cranks and offices Passages or ducts, serving the body.

nerves i.e. muscles or sinews.

weal o' the common Commonwealth.

great toe i.e. Menenius scorns the plebeian.

wise (Ironic).

rascal . . . vantage i.e. notwithstanding his lowly station, the citizen leads the rabble to profit from chaos.

bale Sorrow, harm, destruction.

make . . . subdues him i.e. the citizens' notion of 'virtue' is to honour the corrupt.

garland Hero i.e. the recipient of the laurel wreath, the highest honour.

side factions Take sides.

quarry Heap.

pick Pitch, throw.

persuaded i.e. that they are wrong.

passing Surpassing.

other troop See line 46.

break . . . generosity Break those in authority.

tribunes Magistrates, here to defend the people against the nobles (patricians).

'Sdeath God's death (a form of swearing).

Win upon power Encroach upon the privileges of the nobility.
themes ... arguing Subjects for further argument.
Volsces Longstanding enemies of the Romans. Corioles was fifty miles to the south of Rome.
vent ... superfluity Get rid of the excess, i.e. empty the city of seditious citizens.
Senators The Senate was the governing body of ancient Rome.
by th'ears Fighting.
stiff ... out? Unable to fight?
puts well forth Shows itself well (sarcastic).
gird Laugh at, deride.
The present i.e. may the present.
grown ... valiant His pride detracts from his valour.
nature ... noon i.e. his opinion of himself is further inflated by each success.
giddy censure Foolish criticism.
he i.e. Martius.
demerits Deserts, merits.
all his faults ... honours i.e. the General's mistakes will be referred to as errors Martius would never have committed.
dispatch Preparation.
singularity Personal peculiarity.

Act I Scene 2

Aufidius informs the senators of Corioles of his intelligence that Rome is aware of the Volscian intention to attack.

Commentary

Irritated by the complacency of the senators, Aufidius is aware of the divisions in Rome and presses the urgency of action. In his impatient decisiveness and in what he says of his enemy, Aufidius is presented as the spirited personal rival that we already know Martius is 'proud to hunt' (I,1,234). The scene sustains the tension of expectation established in Scene 1.

enter'd in Aware of.
What i.e. what decisions or intentions.
press'd Impressed, conscripted.
of Rome i.e. by the people of Rome.
great pretences i.e. plan of campaign.
shorten'd Prevented.
set down Lay siege.
the remove The raising of the siege.

parcels Small parts.
only hitherward i.e. to attack Corioles.

Act I Scene 3

In Rome, Volumnia and Virgilia, the mother and wife of Martius, speak of him and await news of the war. Valeria, Virgilia's friend, tells them that she has heard that Cominius has moved to intercept the Volscian army, while Martius and the remainder of the Roman forces are besieging Corioles.

Commentary

The scene introduces the remaining major characters and informs us of the progress of the war. The first citizen's remarks (I,1,38) have prepared us for Volumnia's fierce pride in her warrior son, expressed in language that evokes the violence of his nature. It is with joy and love that she imagines him as 'a thing of blood' (see II,2,109), scything the enemy. Valeria's pleasantries and gentle raillery approve the Roman matron's adoration of her son. The grandson, too, has a 'confirmed countenance' and is 'noble' in his 'father's moods'. Virgilia's sensitivity and sweetness of manner give her a quiet strength; occasionally she permits herself a barbed question or a dry remark. Volumnia's opening speech is addressed to a retiring, preoccupied, fearful daughter-in-law, who refuses to conduct her life as if her husband were not in great danger; the drama here is domestic, but none the less real, and Virgilia's love for Martius is, in its way, as powerful and intense as his mother's. In some ways the simple, private scene, tinged with ironic humour, is in complete contrast to the public formality and cacophony of the streets. The character of Martius, his upbringing, and the forces within him are here presented indirectly. However, in the tension between public ethos and personal emotions, the classical allusions to supra-human grandeur, and the nervous vulnerability to affection, there is a restatement of the theme of what it is that constitutes the Roman state.

comfortable sort Cheerful manner.
gaze Eyes.
person i.e. of fine, handsome appearance.
it i.e. his 'person'.

a cruel war See Act II, Sc. 2. Cominius describes Martius's first exploits in battle, at the age of sixteen.

bound with oak i.e. a garland of oak, a mark of honour for saving the life of a comrade.

surfeit out of action Live safe and comfortably at home.

As . . . bear i.e. the Volsces run away from him like children from a bear.

task'd to mow Hired to reap a field.

Jupiter King of the Roman gods.

than . . . trophy Than gold becomes his monument.

Hecuba King Priam's wife, i.e. the queen of Troy at the time of the siege. Her son Hector led the Trojan defence.

contemning i.e. in contempt of the sword.

manifest housekeepers Real housewives, staying indoors.

A fine spot Fine embroidery.

confirmed countenance Firm character.

mammocked Tore.

crack A rogue (ironical).

want Lack.

Penelope The wife of Ulysses. During her husband's long absence in the Trojan War, she was courted by many suitors. She evaded them by saying that she was making a shroud for Ulysses' father, and at night she undid each day's work.

sensible Sensitive.

disease . . . mirth Spoil our good humour.

Act I Scene 4

Martius and Titus Lartius are before the walls of Corioles. A mile and a half away can be heard the battle where the Roman general, Cominius, meets the Volscian army, led by Aufidius. A sortie of Volscian defenders reverses Martius's attack on the town and, attempting to counter-attack, he is trapped within the walls and is presumed killed. His reappearance, wounded but undaunted, is an inspiration to the Romans who, led by Titus Lartius, enter the city to rescue Martius.

Commentary

This is the first of the scenes of action that conclude the first act – which must be taken together for consideration of their dramatic effect – and in which Martius's heroism dominates the uncertainty and ferocity of war.

Excited by the prospect of action, his first thought is to take the town quickly, then reinforce Cominius in the main encounter. Surprised by the Volscian advance, Martius's anger is reserved for the timidity of his own forces, pestilent cowards to him, whom, ironically, he speaks of threatening with his own sword. His fearlessness is 'Foolhardiness' to them, and they resign him to 'To th'pot'. But, with the example of Martius's courage before their eyes, and the leadership of Titus Lartius, they resume the attack. Lartius's peroration, when he supposes Martius dead, emphasizes the absolute qualities of a soldier who could shake his enemies 'as if the world/Were feverous and did tremble'. The sympathies of the audience are balanced between admiration for the young hero and the understanding that generalship may require more than scorn and self-sacrifice.

spoke i.e. met in battle.
summon i.e. sound the trumpet.
'larum Alarum. The call to battle.
Mars Roman god of war.
smoking swords Reeking with blood.
fielded friends i.e. Cominius and the army in the field of battle.
No . . . little i.e. read 'less' as 'more'. Therefore, no man fears Martius any more than Aufidius does. The double negative is intended to intensify the idea.
break Break out from.
Their noise be our instruction i.e. be guided by the noise.
proof Safe, tested.
disdain . . . thought They are not as cowed as we anticipated.
edge Sword.
the contagion of the south i.e. the diseases that were bred in the heat.
herd of i.e. Martius is enraged.
abhorr'd . . . seen Smelt before seen.
Pluto Roman god of the underworld ('hell').
All hurt behind In the back, i.e. running away.
agued Feverish, trembling.
Mend i.e. your ways.
leave . . . foe Martius threatens his soldiers. (Dramatic irony.)
their wives i.e. their homes.
seconds Followers.
pot Cooking pot i.e. to death.
answer Fight.
sensibly . . . sword i.e. he feels less than his inanimate sword.
bows, stand'st up When the sword bends, Martius does not.
carbuncle entire A perfect ruby (blood-coloured).
to Cato's wish As Cato, a virtuous Roman, would have wished for.
fetch . . . alike Rescue him, or die.

Act I Scene 5

Corioles is taken, though the main battle rages undecided. As the Roman soldiers sack the city, Martius urges the importance of marching to assist Cominius. Titus Lartius is left to make Corioles secure.

Commentary

Furious at the baseness of the citizen-soldiers, Martius itemizes their clumsy greed. Despite his wounds, he insists on leading 'those that have the spirit' to help Cominius and to confront Aufidius, his 'soul's hate'.

murrain Plague.
movers i.e. an ironic reference to fleers: removers, pillagers.
At a cracked drachma A worthless coin, i.e. at nothing.
Irons of a doit Swords worth little.
doublets . . . them i.e. clothes that a hangman would bury with a corpse, rather than keep them for his own profit.
pack up Quit.
physical i.e. it does him good, like a physic (medicine).
page Attendant.

Act I Scene 6

The main army is on the defensive, though far from being routed. Martius arrives, and leads volunteers against the Volsces' strongest troops.

Commentary

Cominius's language is measured and controlled. He steadies his men for the next charge, reminding them of their comrades advancing on the town, and prays for success. The spirit ebbs from the soldiers and the dramatic tension increases, as the messenger arrives with the 'truth' the audience knows to be partial. The appearance of the blood-stained Martius alters the tenor of the scene. Briefly decrying the 'gentlemen' of 'The common file' of whom the messenger has spoken, Martius refuses to dwell on how he 'prevail'd', preferring to press on with a further attack. His curt questions, incisive assessment, urgency, and challenging appeals to honour and patriotism are an inspiration to the army. The audience is aware of his leadership at this point (lines 66–75) and remembers his failure earlier (I,4,30–45). Without Martius, the enterprise would have failed here as in Corioles; the citizens who resent his pride, and the soldiers who grimly dismiss his courage, depend for their existence on a virtue they find too absolute.

Breathe Rest.
by interims . . . gusts In intervals during the fighting, on the wind.
briefly A short while ago.
fronts i.e. the 'face of each section of the army is forward and smiling.
confound Waste.
flay'd Bloody, like a carcass.
stamp Form.
tabor Small drum.
vaward Vanguard, the advance troops.
Antiates Men of Antium, Aufidius's city.
Prove i.e. put ourselves to the test.
balms Soothing ointments, i.e. dressings for wounds.
painting i.e. blood.
person Body, life.
disposition Intention.
inclin'd Suited.
As cause will be obeyed As circumstances dictate.
Make . . . ostentation Cominius encourages them now to do what they have shouted their intention to do.
Divide in all Share our honours.

Act I Scene 7

Titus Lartius instructs the garrison holding Corioles, and leaves to join Cominius and Martius.

Commentary

This scene is a part of the sequence that represents the whole action by dramatizing parts of it. As Titus Lartius carefully directs those entrusted with holding the city, the audience shares with him the sense that, at that very moment and elsewhere, the fate of the Roman army may already have been decided: 'If we lose the field,/We cannot keep the town.'

ports Gates.
centuries Companies of a hundred men.
guider Guide, scout.

Act I Scene 8

Martius and Aufidius meet in battle. Some Volsces arrive to support Aufidius, but Martius drives them all off.

Commentary

The mutual hatred is a rivalry of 'fame'. To a degree each man measures his own worth by the reputation of his enemy (see I,1,230–31). The insults and challenges are adolescent in their swaggering banality; pride is at stake. The personal duel of Martius and Aufidius is central to the play's construction; this fragment sets them at each other's throats in formal combat, and leaves Aufidius humiliated.

Fix thy foot i.e. prepare to fight.
first budger i.e. the first one to move. (See I,6,44.)
mask'd Daubed. (See 'mantled in your own' [blood], I,6,29.)
Wrench ... power Muster your strength.
bragg'd progeny The race you boast of; a reference to the Roman claim to be descended from the Trojans. Hector was the scourge of the Greeks.
condemned seconds Unwanted, shameful support.

Act I Scene 9

The battle won, Cominius publicly praises Martius. Refusing material reward for his service, Martius has, nevertheless, to accept the title 'Coriolanus'.

Commentary

Cominius formally and enthusiastically proclaims the achievements of Martius, and anticipates his triumphant reception in Rome. As commander of the Roman army, Cominius knows the importance of the 'sign' of honour to the well-being of the state. He has to assert his authority to impose the 'addition' on his lieutenant.

The behaviour of Martius is complex, forcing a balance of interpretation. In plain speech and bluff modesty he declares 'I have done/As you have done, that's what I can'; the comparison that follows – between other men's matching of their thoughts by deeds, and the inferred discrepancy between his own conception and action – has an effect opposite to its intent. Martius's evident embarrassment and his unambitious generosity founder when he is pressed, and his mood is once again contemptuous of emotion and humanity. The sardonic belittling (lines 46–7) of his own courage is as crude as the suggestion that what he calls 'acclamations hyperbolical' are 'sauc'd with lies'. Yet when he gives way, he does so with a combination of laconic self-depreciation and reluctant grace; and he asks, in 'pity' for the freedom of a prisoner. Exhaustion erodes magnanimity, and the moment fades; the man's name is forgotten and the gesture is impotent. Martius's name is now 'Coriolanus', the embodiment of Roman virtue – an ideal that, in its extreme form, extinguishes sympathy for the anonymous 'poor host'.

tell thee o'er i.e. if you (Martius) were to be told of 'this day's work'.

shrug i.e. scarcely believe the story.

gladly quak'd i.e. be simultaneously admiring and fearful.

fusty Stale. (See I,1,255.)

say . . . hearts. . . Admit despite their feelings.

morsel i.e. to Martius the battle was a slight matter, after his taking of Corioles.

steed . . . caparison i.e. Martius is the power and strength, the remainder are the harness (saddle-cloth). The metaphor arises from the wager (I,4. See also I,9,60.)

charter . . . blood Prerogative to praise her child.

He . . . act He who has done what he intended has done more than I have. The implication is that Martius has failed to do all that he wanted.

You . . . deserving You shall not snuff out this praise.

traducement Censure.

vouch'd Offered.

tent Remedy; the 'tent' was a linen for probing and dressing wounds; i.e. the wounds would prove fatal.

soothing Flattery.

steel . . . silk As soft as the silk of an obsequious courtier.

ovator One who is praised.

debile Feeble.

As if . . . lie As if I wanted my small achievements exaggerated.

proper Person.

To undercrest . . . power To wear (like a crest) this honour as best I can.

articulate Negotiate.

Act I Scene 10

The Volsces are defeated, and Tullus Aufidius is in hiding.

Commentary

The act and the series of scenes of action end with the dark note of Aufidius's embittered sense of honour, soiled by the invincible superiority of his enemy Martius. Aufidius is exiled from the Volscian town; his valour poisoned, he denies the 'canon' of humanity.

that I am i.e. a man of valour.
Condition ... mercy Here playing on the other sense of the word 'condition' (i.e. quality). What good quality will those who are helpless be seen to have?
emulation Rivalry.
equal force Fairly.
potch Poke.
Embarquements Hindrances.
upon ... guard Protected by my brother.
hospitable canon i.e. laws of hospitality.
south the city mills Outside the city; a contemporary reference to the mills on the south bank of the Thames.

Revision questions on Act I

1 Examine the clash between Martius and the citizens. Exactly how is each party viewed by the other?

2 Why does Menenius relate the fable of the belly? What is his argument? What are the various dramatic effects of the tale?

3 Describe Volumnia's upbringing of Coriolanus.

4 List the details of the sequence of action leading to the taking of Corioles.

Act II Scene 1

Anticipating the successful return of Martius, the patrician Menenius taunts the tribunes, Brutus and Sicinius. The Roman ladies enter, and Volumnia tells Menenius of her son's triumph. Martius arrives, is again proclaimed 'Coriolanus' and greets his family. As he leaves for the Capitol, Brutus and Sicinius express their fear that he may become consul.

Commentary

In Rome the sour debate between Menenius and the tribunes reminds us of the divisions within the state. Menenius is baiting Brutus and Sicinius with the 'enormity' they claim to find in Martius, and he deflects insinuation by heartily confessing his own imperfections. The squabbling is amusing as well as acrimonious. The stately entry of the noble ladies is in contrast to this, and is a preparation for the formality to come. The tribunes wait and watch (and are jeered at by Menenius, l.142). Hooting at the news the exultant Volumnia brings to him, Menenius glories with her, and together they inventory Martius's wounds.

The mood of infectious, domestic pride alters with subtle menace as the trumpets sound (l.155), at 'the ushers of Martius': before him he carries noise and behind him he leaves tears. The meeting with Virgilia is a tender, generous moment; she is the still centre of his turbulent world. The tension of a poignant silence is released by the banter with Menenius. As the party leave the stage, Volumnia's last words are ecstatic with anticipation of the realization of 'the buildings of my fancy'. The 'one thing wanting' is the consulship, and Coriolanus's understanding of the dangers inherent in this expectation is evident: 'I had rather be their servant in my way/Than sway with them in theirs.'

Coriolanus is proud of his reputation and honour, but this is not vainglory. He is ambitious as a soldier, as an ideal warrior in a warrior caste, but he is not ambitious as the world goes; and the last word in the scene is with the factious partisans who have stood sentinel throughout. Brutus parodies the vulgar enthusiasms; Sicinius is apprehensive of a diminution in the tribunes' power. However, they feel that Coriolanus's temper cannot make for consistency, either in reception (l.230) or rule (l.220), and that as his pride makes him vulnerable to provocation, the combination of this and the suggestion to the people of Coriolanus's supposed tyrannical intention (l.243) will produce the fire that 'shall darken him for ever'. With dramatic irony the scene ends with the astonished messenger's account of the incomparable popularity of Coriolanus.

augurer An interpreter of omens.
In . . . in i.e. what fault makes him a 'poor' man.
right-hand file The best men, i.e. patricians. The metaphor is taken
   from the place of honour given traditionally to the finest soldiers.
very . . . occasion i.e. the slightest occurence.
humorous Whimsical; influenced greatly by the body's 'humours', and
   therefore not of moderate temper. (In those days these bodily
   humours were believed to be blood, phlegm, choler and melancholy.)
allaying . . . Tiber i.e. river water to dilute it.
the first complaint i.e. the first case.
tinder-like Hot-tempered.
wealsmen Men of the commonwealth, statesmen (sarcastic).
Lycurguses North's *Plutarch* included a life of the Spartan legislator,
   Lycurgus.
can (Sarcastic).
ass . . . syllables i.e. their speeches are asinine, with too many 'as-es'.
bear with To put up with; like an ass.
deadly Utterly.
good i.e. honest.
microcosm i.e. face.
bisson conspectuities Blind wisdom.
caps and legs i.e. for bowing and scraping; a fawning popularity.
orange-wife Orange seller.
faucet Tap, for a barrel.
rejourn Postpone.
controversy of threepence i.e. litigation over a negligible sum, a
   contested nothing.
party i.e. to a dispute.
mummers Actors.
bleeding Unresolved.
bencher Judge, i.e. magistrate or senator.
botcher A patcher of clothes.
Deucalion The name in Greek mythology for Noah; i.e. since the flood.
God-den God give you good evening.
moon i.e. Diana.
Juno Wife of Jupiter and queen of the gods.
Take my cap i.e. he throws it in the air.
make a lip Sneer.
Galen A Roman doctor of the second century AD; a medical authority
   respected in Shakespeare's time.
empiricutic i.e. an empirical concoction, quackish.
drench Medicine.
'fidiussed Aufidius-ed.
possessed Informed.
cicatrices Scars.
stand for his place i.e. for consul.
Tarquin The last king of Rome, before the Republic.

nervy Sinewy.
***Sennet* (stage direction)** A set of notes giving a ceremonial flourish.
crabtrees i.e. sour-tempered.
be grafted to your relish i.e. made to like you.
change of honours i.e. a changed name, fresh honours.
bleared ... spectacled i.e. those with poor eyes wear spectacles.
Your ... nurse A chattering nurse.
malkin Wench.
lockram Linen.
reechy Dirty.
bulks Constructions projecting from shops.
leads Roofs.
ridges Roof ridges.
variable complexions Various kinds of people.
Seld-shown flamens Priests rarely seen.
vulgar station Place with the common people.
Commit ... kisses Present their carefully arranged complexions to the glare of the sun, (Phoebus, the Roman sun-god).
pother Uproar.
He cannot ... end He cannot carry his honours as he should.
Upon Owing to.
consul One of the two magistrates, appointed annually, and invested with supreme authority.
napless vesture Poor gown; according to Plutarch, the candidate for consulship wore a toga without a tunic underneath it.
miss it Forgo being consul, to avoid the ritual.
but ... nobles But for the pleading demands of the patricians.
good Interest.
suggest Suggest to, prompt.
camels ... war i.e. beasts of burden.
provand Food, 'provender' in return for the work they do.
touch Kindle.
put upon't Provoked to it.
th'time The present.
Have with you I am with you. Let us go.

Act II Scene 2

Coriolanus appears before the elders of Rome. Cominius is invited to speak of Coriolanus's deeds, in support of the proposed consulship. Coriolanus declines to hear himself praised, but returns to be made consul. He asks that he may be excused the customary appearance before the people, but his unwillingness is brushed aside.

Commentary

The officers' detachment contrasts with the demeaning rancour of
Menenius and the tribunes. Sympathies and suspicions are
balanced: Coriolanus may be 'vengeance proud'; or perhaps, in
'noble carelessness' (an ambiguous phrase) he disdains the wiles of
politicians. The second officer's assessment (lines 24–32) of popular
endorsement as a tribute justly earned, and not to be despised, is
one that 'a worthy man' might well share. This private, anonymous
insight into the world of public exchange is an overture to the main
drama: 'Having determin'd of the Volsces, and/To send for Titus
Lartius, it remains' for the senate to elect Coriolanus consul. The
eulogistic tone of a rhetorical introduction is soon jarred by Brutus's
insistence on the theme of Coriolanus's 'value' of the people. The
'pleasing treaty' Sicinius refers to is a futile compromise. The scene
is edgy; Cominius waits, during the rapid crossfire of Menenius and
Brutus, and then waits again, as Coriolanus, the guest of honour,
stalks away from what he construes as flattery: 'I had rather have
one scratch my head i'th'sun/When the alarum were struck than idly
sit/To hear my nothings monster'd.'

Cominius's speech is to the point: It is held/That valour is the
chiefest virtue and/Most dignifies the haver.'

Coriolanus's life has been exemplary, his courage supra-human,
perhaps – by unintentional inference – inhuman, yet for this 'He
covets less/Than misery itself would give.' His nobility is superlative,
but he kicks (l.124) at honours as well as spoils, and his dislike for
posturing inevitably makes it appear that he also kicks at those to
whom, by extension at least, he owes his 'life and services'. The
suggestion that he might 'o'erleap that custom' that 'might well/Be
taken from the people' does not appear to Coriolanus to be a
manifestation of pride. The crux of the play is that Coriolanus
cannot be true to himself while acting the part that is required of
him (l.145).

The echoing shout of 'joy and honour' is ironically counterpoin-
ted by the plotting (see also II, l,243) of Brutus and Sicinius, who
have noted the implications of Coriolanus's remarks (l.145).

cushions (stage direction) A symbol of administrative office.
brave Fine.
vengeance i.e. with a vengeance.
noble carelessness i.e. suggesting his aristocratic contempt for
  dissembling, and also his disregard for common humanity.

waved Wavered.

discover ... opposite Reveal him to be their enemy.

affect Desire, invite.

bonneted Doffed their caps, i.e. made a show of humility.

Lictors (stage directions) Attendants upon Roman magistrates.

gratify Reward.

think ... out Think rather that Rome lacks the wherewithal to requite you than that we lack the will to enforce it.

loving motion i.e. donning the gown of humility and soliciting their approval.

convented Convened.

treaty Proposal.

remember ... people Retain a proper respect for the citizens.

disbenched Moved, i.e. annoyed.

soothed Flattered.

weigh Deserve, i.e. little.

monster'd Exaggerated.

multiplying spawn The people; the lowest classes were known as proletarians – those fit for breeding children.

singly counter-pois'd Matched by anyone.

made a head for Led an army against.

dictator The Roman leader, appointed with absolute power in time of emergency.

Amazonian Beardless; this use of 'Amazonian' refers to the famous female fighters, the Amazons, who were of course beardless.

might act Was of an age to act the part of a woman, i.e. he was very young.

meed Reward.

oak Garland.

lurch'd all swords Robbed all contenders of the chance.

speak him home Do him justice.

fliers See I,4,30–42.

tim'd Marked.

painted Stained with blood.

shunless destiny Inevitable fate.

gan Did.

doubled Redoubled.

fatigate Tired.

reeking i.e. with blood.

spoil Slaughter.

with measure With distinction.

to spend the time to end it i.e. the action is its own reward.

naked i.e. beneath the gown.

voices Votes.

bate Dispense with.

Put ... to't Do not try their patience, or drive them too far.

Your honour ... form Your unquestioned honour with your formal position.

breath i.e. support.
Do not stand upon't Do not make an issue of it.
our purpose to them What we intend for the people.
require them i.e. ask for popular voice.
contemn ... give Condemn the fact that his request depended upon
  their accord.

Act II Scene 3

Coriolanus, wearing the traditional gown of humility, presents
himself to the citizens of Rome, to ask for their concurrence with
the Senate's wish to make him consul. The people are inclined to
approve him, despite his manner; however, when he returns to
the senate house, the citizens, disquieted, are encouraged by the
tribunes to rescind their approval.

Commentary

This scene dramatizes the conflicting forces at work within the
state: the political determination of the patricians, and the
anguished canvassing of the soldier turned politician, the
opportunism of the tribunes and the citizens' raw goodwill.

The citizens are not ill-disposed towards Coriolanus's being
made consul. The tension of Act I Scene 1 has been dissipated
by the war; the people are duly grateful and respectful, aware of
their power and of the responsibility it imposes. The memory of
Coriolanus's contempt for them rankles but, good-naturedly,
they laugh at their own inconsistency rather than dwell on
resentment. The tone of the opening discussion is predomin-
antly jovial, far from the conspiratorial simmering one might
have expected (see II,2,158). Coriolanus's humility is a kind of
quirky self-assertion. Anything less than this he would regard as
despicable self-abasement. The people, made uneasy by his sardonic reversal of ritual, nevertheless give him their approval,
but later report their dissatisfaction to Brutus and Sicinius.

Coriolanus believes himself to have been appointed consul by
the patricians in whose 'addition', in his view, it lies. The 'custom'
he tolerates with such bad grace is an insincerity that he would
dispense with. To him the multitude is 'many-headed', and
therefore has no head. Authority is conferred by birth and
virtue, and does not issue from 'voices'. The gown of humility
becomes a hair shirt that eventually consumes his dignity. He is

truly humiliated by the requirement that he should act the part of flattering the common people to the effect that they should act the part of flattering him for what he has done truly – no more than his duty. Unconvinced of the authenticity of his gesture, he does not attempt to dissemble; the agonized pretence is hastily discharged and, 'knowing myself again', he can change the garments and take himself off. The ambivalence is neither understood nor forgiven by the people. Crudely swamping subterfuge with a protective sarcasm, Coriolanus makes it, inexcusably, a 'free contempt'. The failing is that his pride will not suffer him to submit with dignity; the irony is that his nature is what has been required of him as a soldier. Coriolanus defers to Menenius's judgement of what is 'wholesome' (l.61); the citizens permit Brutus and Sicinius to exacerbate resentment at Coriolanus's equivocal manner. The anonymous citizens reflect on Coriolanus's repetition of 'voices': 'Was not this mocking?' Restrained until this point, the tribunes now goad uncertainty into rebellion.

Brutus is exasperated with what Sicinius terms ignorance or 'childish friendliness' and demands to know how they have appointed a malignant foe to 'Potency' (lines 174–188) and 'sway o'th'state'. Sicinius advises the crowd that they ought to have 'touch'd his spirit' by demanding Coriolanus's promise to love the people: this would either have produced a 'gracious promise', to which he could have been held, or an outburst of 'surly nature' which would have disqualified his candidature. This emphasizing of the citizens' power is enough to incite them to exercise it, retrospectively at least. The tribunes then shrewdly channel these energies. Efficiently, and with masterly duplicity, they encourage the citizens to lay the blame for their own indecisiveness on having put the tribunes' recommendation of Coriolanus before an instinctive recognition of his 'inveterate hate'. Brutus and Sicinius will escape censure for whatever may follow.

The scene invites the audience to consider the nature of the state (lines 16, 75, 100, 116) as well as the nature of Coriolanus (lines 39, 111–123, 130, 185, 193, 256) as irreconcilable opposites: 'Well then, I pray, your price o' th'consulship?'/'The price is, to ask it kindly.'

a power ... to do i.e. we are not free to exercise that power.

to make us ... serve i.e. it will take little to make the patricians think worse of us.

stood up Protested.

abram Auburn.

consent of one direct way Their agreement on a direction.

wedged Lumped.

for conscience' sake i.e. to look after the man.

tricks Jokes.

by particulars Individually.

to such a pace i.e. curb the tongue.

the virtues ... 'em The virtuous teachings that holy men waste upon them.

wholesome Reasonable. Coriolanus takes it in another sense.

A match Done! i.e. like a bargain struck.

stand Agree.

dearer Higher.

be off Doff my cap.

counterfeitly Falsely.

counterfeit Pretend.

bewitchment ... man The wiles of the demagogue.

bountiful In plenty (adverb).

seal Confirm.

wolvish toge i.e. the gown of humility is worn by Coriolanus as the wolf in the proverb wears the sheep's clothing.

Hob and Dick i.e. any man who turns up; (Hob was a country name for Robert).

needless i.e. because the senate have already made him consul.

vouches Votes, confirmation.

antique time Ancient tradition.

o'erpeer Rise above.

moe More.

limitation Time allotted for requesting votes.

official marks Insignia of office.

Anon Can mean 'in the near future'; here the meaning is 'immediately'.

upon your approbation To ratify your position.

Repair Return.

sway Authority.

plebeii Plebeians; the commons.

Standing ... lord Acting on your behalf.

touch'd Tested.

As cause had call'd you up As occasion demanded.

gall'd Exasperated.

article Condition.

aught Anything.

free Undisguised.

heart Spirit.

rectorship Rule.

of On.

sued-for tongues i.e. the 'voices' that were asked for.

piece Join.

therefore For that reason.

safer i.e. sounder.

Enforce Stress; refer to.

took ... portance i.e. took from you a true understanding of what his bearing implied.

Ancus Marcius The fourth king of Rome.

Numa The second king of Rome.

Hostilius Tullus Hostilius, third king of Rome. All these kings were legendary.

Publius and Quintus Shakespeare here puts preliminary information given by Plutarch (in the introduction to his *Life of Coriolanus*) into the mouth of Brutus. Publius and Quintus lived *after* Coriolanus, indeed, the 'conduit' (the Aqua Marcia) was not built until 144 BC. Plutarch opens the story of Caius Martius ('whose life we now intend to write') as follows:

The house of Martians at Rome was of the number of the patricians, out of which hath sprung many noble personages, whereof Ancus Martius was one, King Numa's daughter's son, who was King of Rome after Tullus Hostilius. Of the same house were Publius and Quintus, who brought to Rome their best water they had by conduits. Censorinus also came of that family, that was so surnamed because the people had chosen him Censor twice.

This is an example of Shakespeare's unconcern with historical accuracy. Perhaps he failed even to realize that some of these people lived before Coriolanus and some after, but in any case it is characteristic of him that he lifts his 'source' entire into his play.

censor Magistrate.

Scaling Balancing.

presently Immediately.

drawn Gathered.

This mutiny ... hazard ... greater i.e. better to risk an uprising now than wait for a greater hazard i.e. when Coriolanus is consul.

answer ... The vantage Take advantage.

Revision questions on Act II

1 Examine Cominius's history of Coriolanus. (II,2).

2 Analyse the behaviour of Coriolanus when he stands for consul.

3 Compare the reactions of the citizens and of Brutus and Sicinius to Coriolanus's standing for the consulship.

Act III Scene 1

Talking of the peace that has been made with the Volsces, the patricians are making for the market place for the formalities of Coriolanus's inauguration as consul. The tribunes halt the procession with warnings of the people's violent opposition. Coriolanus speaks of the political dangers to Rome inherent in the concession of power by the patricians, and of the necessity of revoking the authority of the tribunes. Brutus and Sicinius accuse him of treason and send for support. A mob of plebeians enter and a riot ensues; Coriolanus and the patricians succeed in driving them off. Coriolanus is persuaded to retire, and Menenius remains to attempt to pacify the returning crowd and avert civil war. He does so by excusing Coriolanus's faults, whilst reminding the citizens of his service, and proposing that Coriolanus should stand before the people to answer their complaints.

Commentary

The action of this scene follows rapidly on that of the last, and ends anticipating the drama of an 'answer' by Coriolanus. Dramatic tension accumulates as the conflict of interests becomes a surging amorphous anarchy that threatens the cohesion of the state. Consider the recurrent imagery of the body politic, threatened, headless, diseased.

Note that all the gentry enter, as Coriolanus is presumably to be presented in the market place formally as consul chosen by the politicians and the people. The comments on the peace that has been made with the Volsces, and the reminder of Coriolanus's personal rivalry with Aufidius, convey the general assurance of the patricians. The subject of the conversation, peace, and the self-congratulatory tone of the exchange between the three military leaders, has a quality of dramatic irony, given the previous scene, as does Coriolanus's wish for a 'cause' to seek Aufidius in Antium. The conduct of the patricians is not consistent (setting aside for the moment that of Coriolanus). Cominius defends his comrade against the presumption of the tribunes, who have 'abus'd' the people, provoking them to dishonourable discourtesy. Menenius and the anonymous senators are more apologetic, finding the speeches of Coriolanus tactless and inflammatory. Their silence in the face of his challenging analysis is discretion, not disagreement, however. They defend Coriolanus against the assault they feel he precipitated: 'This man hath marr'd his fortune.' There is exasperation, though, in Menenius's 'Could he not speak 'em fair?' Coriolanus is not the realist they would have him; he does not recognize the inescapable conditions of political life. Menenius pleads Coriolanus's merit, but is forced to concede to onslaught: Coriolanus 'has been bred i'th'wars' and 'a limb that has but a disease'. Menenius's warning is that factions will break out, and having appealed for 'process of law', ironically he becomes 'the people's officer'. The patricians have bought time by this, but they seem to understand the nature of Coriolanus and that of the civic quarrel less thoroughly than do the tribunes, whose predictions were correct (II,3,256).

Brutus and Sicinius, moving ostensibly to prevent disorder, speak with a self-righteousness that might be calculated to infuriate Coriolanus. Their 'absolute "shall" ' is indeed an extension of the 'canon' that authorizes them, the kind of majority rule against which Coriolanus warns the patricians. Brutus and Sicinius accuse Coriolanus of treason, after he has urged the patricians to 'throw their power i'th'dust'. This makes him, in theory if not yet in practice, an 'innovator', and provides a legal justification for their demagoguery, their assertion – shown to be as partial a definition as the patrician sense of property and title – that the city is the people. By instructing the mob to lay down their weapons (but not to disperse) the tribunes are temporarily halting rather than reversing a process they have consciously instigated.

For most of the scene, Coriolanus is speaking to his 'nobler friends', and he does so in a powerful rhetoric that measures the force of his argument. He instantly assesses the mechanism of manipulation and draws the inevitable conclusion, that this will 'curb the will of the nobility,' and enforce a democracy that 'cannot rule,/Nor ever will be rul'd'. The argument – if not the language – is that of Act I, Scene 1. The patricians, 'good but most unwise', nourish 'rebellion, insolence, sedition' by admitting the accusation made against the senate (III,1,126; see also

I,1,15). The tribunate is abrogation of responsibility: 'Where gentry, title, wisdom/Cannot but conclude but by the yea and no/Of general ignorance.' The sincerity of Coriolanus's belief and the coherence of his argument stand in stark contrast to the turbulent emotions and volatile action of the scene.

To Coriolanus the democratic gesture is a 'dishonour' because 'true judgement' must be set aside for mere preference and self-interest, and the state, greater than its 'parties' is bereft of 'integrity', 'Not having the power to do the good it would/For th'ill which doth control't.' Coriolanus addresses the patricians to the truth of their motives, when he points to the mere expediency of the initial concessions: 'When what's not meet, but what must be, was law,/Then they were chosen.' The patricians do not believe in the popular will any more than Coriolanus does; they are simply more conscious of 'odds beyond arithmetic'.

made new head Raised fresh troops.
composition i.e. of peace terms.
road Campaign.
ages Lifetime.
To hopeless restitution Beyond recovery.
prank Masquerade.
against all noble sufferance i.e. more than the patricians can endure.
pass'd Been approved by.
children's voices i.e. the voices of those who do not know their own mind.
then At one moment.
You ... teeth You are their spokesman, why can you not control them.
a purpos'd thing An arranged scene.
repined Regretted it.
Time-pleasers Sycophants.
sithence Since then.
Not ... yours Likely to do your business (i.e. rule) better than you.
bound Headed. i.e. to be made consul.
yoke Be associated.
palt'ring Prevarication.
dishonour'd rub Insulting dishonourable objection.
meinie i.e. crew, pack, crowd. Literally, household retainers.
soothing Flattering, deferring.
cockle Proliferating weed. By giving the common people power, 'the honoured number' (patricians) have encouraged the growth of tares (plebeians). (See St Matthew, 13, 24–30). The patricians are good seed, the plebeians bad.
coin words Invent new words.

measles Diseases.

tetter Infect.

Triton A sea-god.

of the minnows i.e. lord of the tiny.

from Away from, i.e. against established rule. In being so definite either the tribunes are exceeding their authority, or it suits the patricians to suggest this.

His absolute 'shall' His imperative 'shall'.

Hydra The serpent of Greek myth. It had nine heads and could grow two where one was struck off.

horn and noise Noisy horn. Triton is Neptune's trumpeter.

turn your current Divert your power.

vail your ignorance Submit in your ignorance.

lenity Mildness (I,1,218).

learn'd i.e. in government.

cushions i.e. seats on the senate.

great'st . . . theirs Their taste is for a blend of voices in which they have the louder say.

graver bench i.e. the more dignified senate.

Greece The home of democracy, and more democratic than Rome.

up Exerting their powers.

confusion Ruin.

Navel i.e. survival. (See Menenius's fable I,1,95.)

touch'd Threatened.

accusation i.e. of a patrician unconcern for the people's welfare (see I,1,78).

All cause unborn With no good reason.

native Origin, inspiration.

frank donation Free gift.

bosom multiplied i.e. the Hydra-headed multitude.

digest Understand, having assimilated it.

poll Number.

debase The nature of our seats Abrogate our responsibilities as members of the senate.

cares Responsible concerns.

double worship i.e. where there are two authorities, the patrician and the plebeian.

omit Overlook.

unstable slightness i.e. the trivial and inconsistent popular will.

barr'd Obstructed.

discreet Discerning, prudent.

doubt Fear or question?

jump Risk.

The multitudinous tongue i.e. the tribunes who are the voice of the people.

lick the sweet that is their poison Taste the power for which they are unfitted and which will ultimately lead them to destroy themselves.

despite Contempt.

bald i.e. literally and metaphorically, bare, slight.

th'greater bench The higher authority, i.e. the senate.

aediles Assistants to the tribunes.

innovator Rebel.

answer i.e. to the charge of treason.

distinctly ranges Stands separate and distinctive, i.e. the buildings of Rome.

th'rock Tarpeian The cliff on the Capitoline Hill was traditionally used for execution of criminals and traitors. It was so called from Tarpeia, faithless daughter of the governor of the citadel, who was flung from this rock by the Sabines.

temp'rately . . . redress Act moderately to right what you would violently alter.

cold Calm, dispassionate.

prudent helps Wise procedures.

tent Treat.

litter'd Sheltered, i.e. like the cattle they are.

will owe another Will give way to another.

tag Mob.

o'erbear . . . bear Surge over what would normally restrain.

patch'd Remedied, i.e. by any means.

vent Utter.

What the vengeance i.e. an emphatic expression.

cry havoc i.e. a signal to plunder and slaughter.

holp Helped.

peremptory Determined urgently.

deserved Deserving.

Jove's own book i.e. it is well known to the gods.

dam Mother i.e. be like a sow eating her own farrow.

suffer Allow.

brand Mark of disgrace.

clean kam Quite perverse.

Merely awry Completely twisted.

tiger-footed i.e. swift.

unscanned Ill-considered.

tie leaden pounds i.e. weights, to slow down the headlong fury.

process i.e. of law.

bolted Refined.

humane Civilized.

our first way As we had initially intended, i.e. to the execution of Martius.

Act III Scene 2

Coriolanus faces his mother's criticism, persuasion and pleading; reluctantly he agrees to return to the market place to make his peace with the plebeians.

Commentary

This scene takes place seemingly moments later in the home of Coriolanus. The uncompromising firmness of his will is gradually eroded. The emphatic monosyllables – 'yet will I still/Be thus to them' – are followed by silences, brief questions, an impatient exclamation, a speech of desperate contradiction, and finally by a sardonic capitulation.

The Roman matron is the dominant voice and presence. With caustic deference she addresses her errant son, who ought to have 'put your power well on/Before you had worn it out' and 'might have been enough the man you are,/With striving less to be so'. The basis of her argument is that 'honour and policy' can be reconciled; that dissembling expediency is the necessary, even laudable, cloak for ambition and the acquisition of power. Volumnia does not distinguish between military strategies and political manipulation; power is all important, and this end justifies any means by which it is achieved. By her argument, Coriolanus owes it to family, friends, class and state to seem to be 'rul'd'. Coriolanus is initially remonstrative, but then Volumnia almost persuades him to the point of action; he rebels again, she hardens, and separates herself from her wilful child: 'Thy valiantness was mine, thou suck'st it from me,/But owe thy pride thyself'. Unconvinced, but overcome by this accusatory withdrawal, Coriolanus agrees rather to do her will than his own.

He will act a part, and he is the only character to recognize the danger in being false to his own nature: 'Lest I surcease to honour mine own truth,/And by my body's action teach my mind/A most inherent baseness.'

Unable to see the flaw in Volumnia's argument, Coriolanus is trapped by his own hostile conception of the plebeians. If they are the enemy, and this is a war, then 'honour' may perhaps equal 'policy'. There is no reflective soliloquizing, however; the drama is public. Coriolanus's sense of truth, and of the degradation of the abuse of trust by word, is one force; his mother's love and expectation, and the pressures of duty are another. His ambivalence is apparent throughout; contemptuous of himself for his concession, he prepares to perform 'Mildly!'

pull ... ears Bring everything down.
present me Sentence me to.
wheel i.e. the wheel to which a criminal was tied for a flogging, in this case fatal.

precipitation Precipice.
thus As I have been, i.e. unyielding.
woollen vassals Servants in coarse garments.
groats An English coin, a fourpenny piece.
congregations i.e. in church.
ordinance Rank.
power Authority, i.e. the consulship.
You might . . . so You might well have retained your authority without having to go so far.
thwartings i.e. the plebeians, who have frustrated Coriolanus's ambition.
Ere . . . you i.e. before Coriolanus had the power, as consul, and could ignore their opposition.
apt Willing, i.e. fitted for submission.
stoop to th'herd i.e. abase himself before the people.
fit Fever.
But . . . speak Except in situations of emergency.
unsever'd Inseparable.
If . . . request If it is honourable in war to dissemble in order to overthrow the enemy, how is it less so in peacetime?
instruction Knowledge, conviction.
matter Feelings.
roted in Your tongue Learned by heart.
bastards . . . truth Words not in keeping with his true feelings.
take in Capture.
dissemble with my nature Pretend to be what I am not.
in this In this I am speaking for.
spend a fawn Make a conciliating gesture.
of what i.e. of the consulship, of Rome.
want Lack, i.e. of fawning.
here be with them Go along with them.
bussing Kissing.
waving Bowing, in every direction.
correcting thy stout heart Forcing himself to behave in a humble manner, when he would like to behave in a proud one.
ripest mulberry . . . handling i.e. ripe, and therefore too soft to be handled.
so far . . . person As far as your personal authority can be extended.
Free Available.
fiery gulf Flaming pit, i.e. hell.
bower i.e. in gentler surroundings, e.g. a garden or a lady's bedchamber.
unbarb'd sconce Unarmoured, i.e. bare, head.
noble Patrician.
single plot One life.
discharge to th'life Perform convincingly.
choired In harmony.

tent ... take up i.e. pitch camp, occupy, in military fashion.
glasses ... sight Eyes.
surcease Cease.
rather feel thy pride ... stoutness Volumnia would rather experience his disastrous pride than ignobly fear his obstinacy.
valiantness ... owe ...thyself Coriolanus has inherited his courage from his mother; his pride he owes to himself alone.
mountebank i.e. fraudently inspire.
Cog Wheedle, cheat.
word Password.
accuse me by invention Invent things to accuse me of.

Act III Scene 3

Brutus and Sicinius prepare for Coriolanus's return, intending to infuriate him by the manner and substance of the charges, and then to confirm by popular acclaim the decreed punishment. Coriolanus enters, pacifically, but the accusation of treason is more than he can withstand, and in the resulting uproar he is sentenced to banishment.

Commentary

The final movement of the political crisis takes place in public. Sicinius and Brutus shrewdly and efficiently rehearse the forthcoming drama. Their principal charge is that Coriolanus 'affects/Tyrannical power' – the tribunes' interpretation of his urging the patricians to 'throw their power i'th'dust' (III,1,169). Should this fail to 'put him to choler straight' it will be followed by the absurdly false (see I,9,37–40 and II,2,124–9) inference that the common distribution of plunder has been corruptly delayed. This is indeed accusation 'by invention'. With the news that Coriolanus will come to stand trial, there is just time for a review of the arranged voting and issuing of instructions to the Aedile for the direction of the plebeians. The tribunes are confident in their manoeuvring of the people and in their prediction of Coriolanus's wrath. They may believe that they are protecting a legal framework – 'the old prerogative' and a 'season'd office' that is opposed by 'strokes' – but there is little justification in the play for their claims (I,1,209 and III,1,166–7). Their abuse of power is as much the antithesis of democracy as the imagined tyranny against which they claim to be a bastion. The charge of treason is an exaggeration; Coriolanus is primarily accused of an intention that may be inferred from his language and conduct. The effective commuting of punishment from death to banishment may be interpreted as a 'noble' (see l.143 and also l.39) gesture, or a carefully timed reduction of the extreme to the practicable. Brutus's equating (by implication, l.84) of Coriolanus's 'service' with his own, the silencing of Cominius, and the encouragement of the mob to humiliate Coriolanus support the latter view.

Coriolanus at the moment of his fall seems largely an innocent victim of chicanery. As the patricians and plebeians face one another he prays for the conditions indispensable for the safety of the state: justice, love, peace. To Sicinius's 'demand' that he 'submit' to the people, 'allow' their officers and 'suffer lawful censure', Coriolanus replies 'I am content'. Characteristically uneasy at Menenius's emotive references to battle scars, Coriolanus dismisses this attempt to ingratiate him and assumes the initiative only to relinquish it: when directed to 'Answer to us', instead of making demands himself, Coriolanus's reply is conciliatory. Being called a traitor by the people by whom, if anything (I,4,34–6; I,6,43–5), he has felt betrayed, is more than he can temperately bear. The contempt is initially principled: 'I would not buy/Their mercy at the price of one fair word'; then it degenerates to the scathing, insulting invective of lines 120–24, reminiscent of Act I, Scene 1. The virulence is understandable in the sense that it is an expression of defiance, but tragically inexcusable in its being a denial of humanity, that demeans the speaker more than those he decries. Coriolanus's banishment of the people is committing them to the charge of their own feeble ignorance, his declaration that 'There is a world elsewhere' has a petulant, absurd, hubristic quality, but it may also arouse pity for the rejected hero and make the audience fear for the jubilant citizens.

charge him home Press your charges as forcefully as you can.
affects Desires.
evade us there i.e. rebuffs these charges successfully.
Enforce Accuse.
envy Malice.
the spoil got on the Antiates Booty from the campaign against the men of Antium.
set down by th'poll i.e. naming the voters.
tribes North: 'The people would proceede to geve their voyces by

Tribes (territorial districts or constituencies, favouring a popular vote), and not by hundreds (centuries, subdivisions of classes discriminated by wealth to give patrician control); for by this means the multitude of the poore needy people . . . came to be of greater force.'

'I'th'right and strength o'th'commons' According to the rights and by the power.

old prerogative i.e. what Sicinius refers to as an old-established right.

Put him to choler straight Immediately anger him.

his worth Of contradiction i.e. either opportunities to speak his mind, or establish a reputation by opposition.

chaf'd . . . temperance Once he is roused he cannot speak moderately.

looks Promises.

piece Coin.

Will . . . volume Will stand being called a knave any number of times.

shows of peace Ceremonies, orderly conduct.

Audience Hear!

no further . . . present With no more, and on no other occasion?

determine Be determined.

envy you i.e. express malice to you, or resent your power.

Answer i.e. answer the charge against you; do not question us.

season'd i.e. established by tradition, or so Sicinius claims.

fold Enfold.

injurious Insulting.

free Open, honest.

Tarpeian death See textual note p.43; 'th'rock Tarpeian', (Act III, Scene 1).

check my courage Restrain my spirit.

Envied against Been ill-disposed towards.

not Not only.

dreaded i.e. to be feared, respected.

distribute Administer.

estimate Reputation.

cry Pack.

finds not till it feels Finds nothing out except by harsh experience.

Making but Leaving only.

deliver you i.e. ignorance gives you up.

Abated Defeated.

despite Contempt.

vexation Torment.

Revision questions on Act III

1 Analyse Coriolanus's arguments opposing the tribunate. (III,1)

2 How does Volumnia persuade Coriolanus to return to the tribunes and the people? (III,2)

3 How do the tribunes manoeuvre Coriolanus into a position of disadvantage, and eventually banish him? (III,3).

Act IV Scene 1

Coriolanus bids farewell to his family and friends, and leaves Rome, alone.

Commentary

In this moving scene Coriolanus is at his best. Calm, dignified, and ironically resigned to banishment, he comforts those who mourn his departure. Conscious of their love, he recommends to them the consolations of philosophy (lines 3–9, 26–27). As he turns from one to another, the pathos is intensified by Volumnia's bitterness and her anxiety, Virgilia's silent grief, the paternal comradeship of the older men; and most particularly by the spirit of Coriolanus as he enters the moral anarchy of exile, away from family, friends and community, 'alone/Like to a lonely dragon that his fen/Makes fear'd and talk'd of more than seen', proudly determined on a constancy belied by the latent menace of this dominant image.

beast ... away i.e. the people, see II,3,16–17 and III,1,92.
extremities ... spirits Misfortunes tested character.
fortune's blows ... cunning i.e. when fortune strikes at a nobleman ('gentle' means noble, and is opposed to 'common' 1.5) the blows must be withstood by what is truly noble in his spirit ('cunning' means wisdom, insight).
load ... precepts Instruct me morally.
conn'd Learned.
red pestilence Possibly typhus fever.
Hercules A reference to the twelve labours of Hercules. If Volumnia had been his wife, she would have performed half.
fond Foolish.
wot Know.
exceed the common Do more than an ordinary man can.
cautelous Deceitful.
practice Trickery.
exposure Exposure.
starts Starts up, suddenly appears.
repeal Recall.
advantage i.e. the advantage of the moment.
needer i.e. the one who might profit from the advantage, Coriolanus.

Act IV Scene 2

Returning from the gates of Rome, Volumnia, Virgilia and Menenius meet Brutus and Sicinius.

Commentary

The tribunes, having succeeded in their intentions, are now cautious and apprehensive. Volumnia, feeding on her anger, berates Brutus and Sicinius as they try to scurry away. This scene shifts our sympathies further towards Coriolanus in his adversity, and also reminds us of the differences that remain and fester in a divided Rome. Volumnia's indomitable, vengeful spirit evokes the absent Coriolanus, and prepares us for the drama of their final meeting.

mad Furiously angry.
hoarded plague i.e. the stored vengeance of Heaven.
Will you be gone? i.e. Brutus moves away, but Volumnia does not.
mankind Sicinius is questioning the propriety of Volumnia's virulence; she takes up the word in the sense of human kind.
foxship i.e. the ungrateful cunning.
wise words Volumnia means this sarcastically.
Arabia i.e. a desert, outside the law.
tribe Family.
posterity i.e. the tribune's future – his family.
noble knot i.e. the bond with Rome.
Cats i.e. the rabble; creatures, vile things.
mysteries i.e. mysteries of life.
have Permit.
baited Harassed.
starve with feeding Either die from what I consume or, simply, go hungry.
puling Crying. Volumnia is speaking to Virgilia.
Juno-like Like the chief goddess of the Romans, the wife of Jupiter, celebrated for her anger.

Act IV Scene 3

A Roman and a Volscian meet by chance on the road between Rome and Antium. The Roman is a traitor – a spy for the Volsces – and he speaks of the prospect of civil war in Rome. The Volscian tells him of the mobilization of the Volscian army.

Commentary

These two cheerful mercenaries appear only at this point in the play. The function of the scene is to create a sense of treachery and duplicity, to suggest the passing of time between Coriolanus's banishment and his appearance in Antium, to stress the weakness of Rome and the advantage its enemy can make of this; and it is also an interlude between the primary political section of the play and the final movement of enmity and reconciliation – to which it also serves as a prelude.

services against 'em i.e. the man is a traitor, a spy for the Volsces.
favour ... tongue Identity is apparent from your speech. ('favour' means face).
a note Instructions.
He cannot choose i.e. he must appear well.
distinctly billeted Separately enrolled.
in th'entertainment Being paid, by implication, mobilized.

Act IV Scene 4

In Antium Coriolanus seeks out the house of Aufidius.

Commentary

The stage directions explicitly require Coriolanus to be meanly apparelled, reduced to the condition to which the humiliation of exile has condemned him. At the risk of his life he places himself at the mercy of his rival – no more curious a reversal than his rejection by the Rome he served. Alone, virtually for the first time in the play (see II,3,111), he soliloquizes, in self-justification rather than in self-examination, on the fickleness of fortune. This is far from the stoic calm of Act IV Scene 1. Coriolanus the Roman no longer exists; banishment has put him beyond allegiance, and time and loneliness have eroded his humanity so that he has become 'a kind of nothing' (V,1,11–15), and with tragic irony he can only assuage his sense of betrayal through identification with his great enemy, and by his own betrayal of all that he has loved: 'My birthplace hate I, and my love's upon/This enemy town.'

'fore my wars Under my onslaught.
slippery turns Changes of fortune.

dissension of a doit Quarrel over a trifle.
fellest Fiercest.
broke their sleep i.e. consumed them.
interjoin their issues Either, act jointly, or, permit their children to marry.

Act IV Scene 5

Coriolanus presents himself at Aufidius's house and reveals his identity, demanding either service with the Volsces, or death. Aufidius welcomes Coriolanus, makes him joint commander of the Volscian forces, and gives him a place of honour at the Volscian banquet. The servants who witness this then comment on the irony of events.

Commentary

The words 'service', 'name', 'noble' recur in this scene, calling attention to Coriolanus's inversion of values.

A disguised, muffled figure, whose proud manner intimidates the serving men trying to shoo him away, Coriolanus is now merely a shell. Stripped of honour and rank by the 'dastard nobles' of a 'canker'd' and 'thankless' country, he almost invites death at the hands of his enemy. Acting from blind compulsion, and not reflection, Coriolanus plainly states his misery and presents his throat to the enemy: 'Which not to cut would show thee but a fool'. At first Aufidius does not know Coriolanus. Moved by the drama of an appeal that is also a challenge, Aufidius venerates Coriolanus, giving over half his own commission. This gesture, paradoxical and emotional, is a flat contradiction of expectation, and also a reminder of the intimacy of the soldiers' rivalry; the proud submission of Coriolanus is accepted by Aufidius as a kind of tribute to the valour that was poisoned (Act I, Scene 10) by defeat.

The servants' gossip is light relief in a scene of intense emotion. Also, these ordinary mortals remind us of the precarious balance between love and hate, of the mutability of reputation (Act IV, Scene 7); and the realism of their remarks on war and peace is a striking commentary on the whole action and theme of the play: 'peace ... makes men hate one another ... Reason: because they then less need one another.'

avoid Leave, get out.
batten Grow fat.
canopy Sky.
kites and crows i.e. carrion birds, of the battlefield.
daws Jackdaws, i.e. dolts, as this bird was thought to be foolish.
meddle Interfere. Coriolanus deliberately takes it in a sexual sense.
prat'st Speak foolishly.
trencher Wooden plate.
tackle Dress, appearance.
vessel Body, and, by implication, character.
memory Memorial.
the rest i.e. of me, of my character and reputation.
Whooped Jeered (III,3,137–8).
full quit Revenged fully.
wreak Vengeance.
maims of shame Shameful wounds, i.e. suffered by the country.
under Infernal.
tuns Barrels.
Jupiter ... true i.e. thunder; thought to be a sign of Jupiter's agreement.
grained ash Lance.
clip Embrace.
The anvil of my sword i.e. Coriolanus's body, which Aufidius has
  struck before like an anvil.
Mars Aufidius addresses Coriolanus as the god of war.
target Shield.
several Separate.
down together Brought down fighting.
Unbuckling helms Unfastening helmets.
bowels The metaphor suggests evisceration.
O'erbear't Overbear it, like floodwater.
commission Authority and, by implication, forces.
set down Determine.
set up Spin.
lief Willingly.
wont to thwack Used to beat.
carbonado A piece of meat, scored across for broiling.
bald Bare-headed.
sanctifies himself i.e. considers Coriolanus a source of holiness.
turns ... discourse Listens adoringly to everything he says.
sowl Seize.
polled Cleared.
directitude Possibly discreditude or dejectitude is meant here.
crest Head; like the crest of a bird, or the plume of a helmet.
conies Rabbits.
vent Rumour, clamour.
mulled Stupefying, mild.
They are rising i.e. from the table.

Act IV Scene 6

News that the Volsces, led by Coriolanus, are attacking Rome
disrupts the peace of the city and the tribunes' peace of mind.

Commentary

Brutus and Sicinius are congratulating themselves on having
'tradesmen singing in their shops and going/About their function friendly.' Even Menenius agrees that all is well. The citizens
give thanks to their leaders, who accept this as a tribute to their
virtue, measuring their own fitness for office by Coriolanus's
regrettable inadequacy (lines 27–37). The complacency almost
invites disorder.

A succession of messengers reports the news of war, and the
effect is ironical and cumulative. The first messengers are dis-
missed as rumour-mongers, their words a feeble deception in
the face of possibility: 'He and Aufidius can no more atone/
Than violent'st contrariety'.

Images of fire and destruction accumulate, and a sense of
panic takes hold as Cominius confirms the voice of a 'slave'.
Coriolanus 'is their god. He leads them like a thing/Made by
some other deity than nature.' Bitterly sarcastic, Cominius and
Menenius face the tribunes with the success of their political
handiwork. Both of the patricians, fearful as they are for Rome,
see a just revenge in Coriolanus's denial of the country that
betrayed him. They blame themselves rather than Coriolanus.
Then, to complete the discomfiture of the tribunes, the citizens
remember their own earlier confusion, and dissociate themselves from decisions that were taken in their name.

His remedies i.e. the actions that were necessary to remedy the
 'disease', Coriolanus.
tame i.e. the disturbances are over.
make his friends Blush Embarrass the supporters of Coriolanus, i.e.
 because his absence is no loss.
pest'ring Crowding.
stood to't Were resolute in opposing Coriolanus's consulship.
affecting . . . assistance Intending to establish himself as
 unquestionable dictator.
rumourer whipped i.e. punished for bringing unwelcome news.
coming Emerging.
raising Rumour-mongering.

spacious General.

The young'st and oldest thing i.e. enveloping all, the young and the old.

atone Be at one.

O'erborne their way Overborne (like a flood) what lay in their way.

leads Roofs.

to your noses Before your faces.

franchises Rights.

an auger's bore Tiny hole made by an auger.

your apron-men i.e. the tradespeople who supported you.

voice i.e. votes.

Hercules . . . fruit A reference to the eleventh of the twelve labours of Hercules – the picking of the golden apples of the three daughters of Hesperus.

smilingly revolt Desert Rome for Coriolanus.

something i.e. to respect.

charg'd Would urge (attack).

fair hands A fair mess of matters.

S'incapable of help So incapable of remedy.

clusters Crowds.

roar i.e. for mercy.

second name Second to Coriolanus in reputation.

obeys his points i.e. Coriolanus's every order.

cast . . . caps Cf. III,3,137.

coxcombs Fools' heads.

Act IV Scene 7

Aufidius's lieutenant reports Coriolanus's success and popularity. Aufidius regrets earlier generosity and, in analysing his rival's character, predicts Coriolanus's fall.

Commentary

Like the battle scenes in Act I, the setting is indeterminate. The conversation returns us to Aufidius during the campaign against Rome. One of the impressions created is that of time passing and events moving towards resolution; with dramatic economy not all that occurs is seen by the audience, but takes place offstage in a world that seems to have an independent existence.

Aufidius's reversion to his former hatred is true to his emotional nature, and is prefigured by his own words (Act I, Scene 10), by the chatter of his servants (IV,5,196–219), and even by the political acuity of Brutus and Sicinius when speaking to

Coriolanus and Cominius (I,1,260–75). Aufidius darkens Coriolanus's future by the oblique menace of 'he knows not/What I can urge against him', and by the enigmatic 'yet he hath left undone/That which should break his neck or hazard mine'. Aufidius also gives an objective assessment of the indissoluble combination of factors that have led to Coriolanus's expulsion. He cites 'pride', 'defect of judgement' or 'nature/Not to be other than one thing', and he refers to the immutable nature of political relations in themselves: 'So our virtues/Lie in th'interpretation of the time.' To Aufidius authority is merely a function of power: 'One fire drives out one fire, one nail, one nail;/Rights by rights falter, strengths by strengths do fail.' This is a powerful, bleak scene, close to soliloquy. It is a reflection on the elusive essence of the tragedy.

darken'd Obscured.

lame the foot Impede.

changeling Traitor.

your particular Your sake.

husbandry Management.

left undone i.e. left Aufidius alive? The meaning is never made clear.

sits down Lays siege.

osprey Fish-hawk. The osprey was supposed to fascinate fish, so that they lay on their backs – an easy prey.

honours even i.e. the honours he received were more than he could cope with (II,1,222–4).

disposing Taking advantage.

casque Helmet, i.e. field of battle.

cushion i.e. senate house.

austerity and garb Austere manner.

spices Elements.

it Criticism, if the antecedent of 'it' is 'one of these', i.e. a fault. Thus the faults are seen as inseparable from the virtues that are praised. If 'it' is taken as referring to 'merit', then there is still a suggestion that the proclamation of merit tends to detract from it. This leads into the lines that follow.

power ... done i.e. power, commendably exercised is snuffed out (tomb) by fame and consequent defamation (from the formal rostrum of a 'chair'). So public acclaim is ultimately pejorative.

One fire ... fail i.e. the proverbial wisdom that one force will give way to a greater.

Revision questions on Act IV

1 What is the condition of Rome after the banishment of Coriolanus?

2 What is the dramatic function of Act IV, Scene 2?

3 Describe the appearance of Coriolanus before Aufidius, and account for the latter's reaction.

4 Carefully consider Aufidius's estimate (in Act IV, Scene 7) of the character of Coriolanus.

Act V Scene 1

Cominius has returned unsuccessful from his audience with Coriolanus. Menenius, encouraged by the tribunes, thinks that he might be better received.

Commentary

The images of Coriolanus are of a savage god, destroying the innocent together with the guilty in the fire of his revenge. The unity of the group of 'others', tribunes and patricians, is jarring. Cominius is in fact reporting to all his fellow countrymen – his concern is for Rome – that he finds hope only in the appeal to be made by Volumnia and Virgilia 'For mercy to his country'. Once again Menenius takes bitter pleasure in reviling Brutus and Sicinius for the 'good work' which will burn him as well as them. With characteristic complacency he undertakes to speak to Coriolanus, explaining away Cominius's reception by the fact that Coriolanus 'had not din'd'. Menenius has a feeble understanding of what has happened; his speeches are a pathetic recall of aborted relationships and names that are now meaningless to the 'titleless' Coriolanus. Cominius is a grim realist, and he makes Menenius's nostalgic optimism seem illusory.

This scene retrospectively dramatizes one plea and prepares us for two more: Menenius's deputation, which we already sense must be a failure, and the final tragic meeting of Volumnia and Coriolanus.

his general Coriolanus's general, i.e. Cominius.
knee i.e. crawl.
coy'd Was coy, i.e. reluctant.

wrack'd for Rome i.e. destroyed Rome; wrecked it, or put it on the rack.

bare Beggarly.

pick ... pile ... chaff Pick out individual grains from the mouldy husks, i.e. spare the city for the sake of a few. (See also I,1,16 and 225).

nose th'offence i.e. smell the offensive chaff.

In ... help At this time, when help was never needed more.

instant army ... make Any army we can raise at the moment.

unkindness Unnatural behaviour.

hum i.e. express dissatisfaction.

taken well Spoken to at the right time.

din'd ... conveyances ... fasts The extended reflection echoes the fable of the belly (I,1,134–9). The belief was that digested food became blood that was then conveyed to the limbs by veins.

dieted Conditioned.

in gold In a chair of gold, i.e. in majestic state.

injury The injustice done him.

What ... conditions Coriolanus sent a letter after Cominius stating several conditions, the acceptance of which Coriolanus had sworn to. (A disputed passage).

Unless i.e. unless we hope.

Act V Scene 2

Menenius arrives at a Volscian camp some distance from Rome. Coriolanus turns him away.

Commentary

It is Menenius's turn to be taunted. Melodramatically he announces himself as 'an officer of state', one whose name should mean something to the guards. But the 'virtue' of his name is nothing to the Volscians. In a speech in which he admits, and even compliments himself on, his verbosity and enthusiasm for legitimate exaggeration, he betrays the patrician conception of Coriolanus as a figure whose 'fame unparallel'd' can be 'haply amplified'. The form of his address to his friend has the absurdity of an over-rehearsed declaration: 'The glorious gods sit in hourly synod about thy particular prosperity'. The sentimental self-abasement of 'old father Menenius' is crushed by Coriolanus's one word, 'Away!' The silence of the old man as Coriolanus dismisses him is made more moving by the over-confident blundering that preceded it. His departure is dignified: 'He that hath a will to die by himself, fears it not from another: let your general do his worst.' Momentarily, at least, he is a 'noble fellow', and comedy has become pathos.

Coriolanus appears relentless, unmoved by the appeal of the man who has been almost a father to him. His affairs are 'servanted' to others, and revenge negates the claims of 'Wife, mother, child'. Aufidius drily notes the irony in the second watchman's words: 'the rock, the oak not to be wind-shaken'. Notwithstanding such clarities, the scene is subtly paradoxical in ways that work against the surface movement of the narrative. Intellectual sympathies may be with the sardonic first watchman's view that: 'you have pushed out your gates the very defender of them, and, in a violent popular ignorance, given your enemy your shield'. Menenius's 'palsied intercession' makes him a 'decayed dotant', half a man. The patrician pride of his exit, however, retrieves his humanity. The claims are real – for all the pomposity of the utterance.

The 'constant temper' of Coriolanus is perhaps just that; Aufidius may have said more than he knows. Coriolanus is proud of the strength of his feeling: 'Mine ears against your suits are stronger than/Your gates against my force'. But the references of his own argument reveal a suppressed awareness of what is natural. Friendship with Menenius cannot (lines 84–5) command Coriolanus's pity because of the poison of Rome's ingratitude. Coriolanus's nature is therefore human: the reaction against injustice is what has suppressed other feelings that are truer in a moral sense to his nature. In the first two scenes of this last act, with all the suggestion of the immutability of Coriolanus, a nemesis of purgatorial fire, there is also a clear statement of humanity that prepares us for Coriolanus's ultimate response to the appeal of the women. When Cominius knelt before him, ''Twas very faintly he said "Rise"' (V,1,66); and, having told Menenius to be gone, Coriolanus concedes 'Yet, for I lov'd thee,/Take this along; I writ it for thy sake'.

lots to blanks i.e. tickets e.g. for a lottery; 'blanks' would not win prizes. Menenius means that the probability is that the soldiers have heard of him.

virtue Worth.

lover Good friend.

verified . . . suffer Supported my friends, of whom he is the greatest, with the highest praise that truth would bear.

subtle Tricky.

tumbled ... throw i.e. rolled (spoken) further than was intended.
stamp'd the leasing Sealed a falsehood.
palms i.e. hands raised in supplication.
palsied intercession Trembling plea.
decayed dotant Senile creature.
an errand A report, i.e. I will deliver the message for you.
Jack guardant i.e. a puffed-up sentry.
office me i.e. officiously keep me away.
Guess Judge.
entertainment with Treatment by.
swound Swoon.
synod Conference. i.e. let the gods continually protect you.
water i.e. Menenius's tears.
hardly With difficulty.
block i.e. literally an obstruction; also blockhead.
Though ... breasts My revenge is my own, but the power of remission
lies with the Volsces ('My affairs/Are servanted', lines 80–81).
familiar Friends.
Ingrate forgetfulness i.e. that of Rome to Coriolanus is the cause of his
to Menenius.
shent Upbraided.

Act V Scene 3

Virgilia, Volumnia, Valeria and young Martius present themselves to Coriolanus in the Volscian camp, to plead for their city.
Coriolanus is persuaded by his mother to make peace. The
ladies retire to Rome while Coriolanus returns with Aufidius to
answer to the Volscian senators.

Commentary

This powerful, moving scene is the climax of the play. The
appeal from Cominius for Coriolanus to spare the city, and
Menenius's appeal to old allegiance and friendship, have failed
to move Coriolanus, from his course at least. The ultimate
appeal, from his family, to the closest of all human ties, does still
the metallic clamour of the action, and Coriolanus is finally
aware that he is no more than a man.

The struggle is over the future of his country, and for the lives
of his friends and loved ones. Most dramatically and tragically, it
is for Coriolanus himself, in an inner, spiritual sense. To act as
he intends, he must deny 'Great nature', break all natural bonds
of affection and stand isolated and untouchable, 'As if a man

were author of himself/And knew no other kin'. The latent
uncertainty of Coriolanus's opening remarks to Aufidius, and
the evident distress of the soliloquy (lines 22–37) show that this is
never likely.

All Coriolanus's reactions point to the inevitability of the
moment of concession: the tenderness of his greeting of Virgilia,
with a kiss 'Long as my exile, sweet as my revenge!'; the
graciously phrased refusal to allow the 'most noble mother of
the world' to kneel to her 'corrected son'; the courteous acknowledgement of Valeria, a symbol of innocence and purity; and the
loving prayer that his son may be all that the father is, 'a great
sea-mark, standing every flaw/And saving those that eye thee!',
and more perhaps – 'To shame unvulnerable'. The attempt to
persevere with the 'unnatural scene' is concluded by Coriolanus's returning from greeting the family he may be about to
destroy to sit in a chair of state (V,1,63 and V,3,131), sur-
rounded by Volscian allies, and hear out the 'colder reason' of
the suitors.

Volumnia reminds him of what condition his actions have
brought his family to, and how this opposition of 'mother, wife
and child' by 'son, husband and the father' can only be an
evisceration of himself and his country. Threatening suicide, she
identifies her existence with that of Rome, and Virgilia breaks
her silence and weeping to say that this is true also for her. The
pathetic defiance of the child completes the separation. Coriolanus, not for the last time in the scene (l.168), has to turn
aside to retain his composure: 'Not of a woman's tenderness to
be,/Requires nor child nor woman's face to see.' Volumnia's
rhetoric now assumes a subtlety distinctly reminiscent of Act III,
Scene 2. Reconciliation, not war, will bless both the Volsces and
the Romans. The basis of the appeal is that Coriolanus's honour
cannot be defiled by generosity that will ensure the nobility of
his 'name'. His 'fine strain' of honour, Volumnia suggests, is a
petty imitation of the gods, if Coriolanus cannot forgive:
'Think'st thou it honourable for a noble man/Still to remember
wrongs?' He has no answer. The lines that follow are less rhetorical in tone than personal, and they constantly remind Coriolanus of the son's duty to the mother. Accusing him of a
vaunted pride that suffocates pity, she challenges him to spurn
her request as unjust, and once more kneels, and in her most
effective final stroke, inextricably linking personal and political

ties, she denies that he is her son and threatens a dying curse:

This fellow had a Volscian to his mother;
His wife is in Corioles, and his child
Like him by chance. Yet give us our dispatch:
I am husht until our city is afire,
And then I'll speak a little.

The figures kneeling before a throne make a silent tableau in the hiatus required by the specific stage direction, '*Holds her by the hand silent.*' In this moment Coriolanus is freed by his love from the unnatural diminution of a vengeful self. This stirring of human feeling is also fatal to him, as he only is aware. Volumnia has either not understood or not admitted to herself that what she advocates involves duplicity – the breaking of Coriolanus's word to the Volsces. Philosophically, Coriolanus accepts his fate – 'let it come' – and pursues a peace that he must now excuse as being convenient to the state in which he has taken service. The calmness of his speech as Coriolanus takes what will be his last leave of his family suggests inner tranquillity after turmoil. The theme is a 'peace' (l.209) from which Coriolanus is excluded by the abiding enmity of Aufidius, and the danger of having set 'mercy' and 'honour' supposedly 'At difference'.

Set down our host Prepare to besiege the city.
My partner i.e. Aufidius.
plainly Straightforwardly, honestly.
general i.e. public suit, for mercy.
private whisper i.e. the particular pleas of family and friends.
grace Show respect to; humour.
All bond and privilege of nature break! i.e. all natural ties and human affections.
eyes i.e. Coriolanus's outlook has changed.
out i.e. run out of words.
virgin'd i.e. he has remained faithful to her love.
impression i.e. in the earth, of Coriolanus's kneeling to his mother.
Show ... parent i.e. Volumnia ironically implies that she acts unnaturally in kneeling to her child, when 'duty' requires the reverse.
corrected Rebuked.
Fillip Strike.
Murd'ring impossibility Making the impossible happen.
curdied Congealed.
Dian's temple Diana, goddess of chastity and the moon.
poor epitome ... yourself i.e. the child is a copy, which, in the fulness of time, may show like his father.
The god of soldiers Mars.

inform Inspire.

stick Stand out.

sea-mark A point of reference, on land, by which sailors take bearings.

flaw Gust of wind.

The thing . . . denials i.e. what I have sworn never to grant cannot therefore be a denial of a request.

capitulate Come to terms.

mechanics Common labourers.

our raiment . . . bodies i.e. their clothing and their general condition are indication of their suffering.

bewray Reveal.

capital Deadly.

bear the palm i.e. carry the symbol of victory.

than to Than that you will.

Trust to 't, thou shalt not Volumnia is threatening to commit suicide.

Not . . . see i.e. to avoid being overcome by tender, feminine feelings, I must not look on their faces.

whose chronicle thus writ i.e. the story of your name thus written.

fine strains Refined sense.

graces Qualities; then illustrated ironically with reference to Coriolanus.

charge Load.

sulphur Lightning.

rive Split.

stocks i.e. a prisoner babbling inconsequentially.

fond of Wanting.

restrains't Withhold.

reason Argue.

Like him by chance i.e. Coriolanus being a Volscian, the child's resemblance is illusory.

husht Silent.

gods . . . laugh i.e. at the ironies of human folly.

unnatural scene i.e. the opposition of son (and husband and father) to the kneeling mother (and wife and child).

true wars i.e. according to his undertaking.

convenient i.e. a peace that benefits both parties.

work . . . fortune i.e. manipulate affairs so that I may return to my former position of authority and prestige.

better witness i.e. formal terms of peace.

Act V Scene 4

In Rome Menenius is telling Sicinius of the futility of any further embassy to Coriolanus, when news comes of the citizens' arrest of Brutus. As another messenger brings word of the peace, the popular celebration of it can be heard.

Commentary

This scene and the next one are in dramatic contrast to Act V, Scene 3. After the silence, there is a cacophony of rejoicing. The noises off-stage were intended to be the loudest and most exultant that the Elizabethan theatre could produce. The dominant image is of a returning, joyous populace, saved from imminent destruction, rushing like waters compressed by wind and tide. The emotive release is infectious.

Before this, however, the dramatic irony of Menenius's self-indulgent pessimism reminds us of the pride of Coriolanus, the 'dragon', the 'engine', sitting in state, wanting 'nothing of a god but eternity and a heaven to throne in', the moment before the 'mercy' he is assumed to lack is trumpeted to Rome. In despair, Sicinius prays to the gods to turn aside what Menenius irascibly refers to as a fatal wrath for which Rome must bear the collective responsibility. Meanwhile, the changeable citizens are preparing to execute Brutus, as the architect of their doom. The shouting of those who 'Make the sun dance' naturally moves the audience, but silence (V,3,183) is not forgotten.

yond coign Yonder corner-stone.
If it be i.e. it is impossible, therefore there is no hope.
condition Character.
horse i.e. than a horse remembers its dam.
engine i.e. of war. e.g. battery ram or catapult.
corslet Body armour, made of steel.
hum ... battery i.e. his manner of speaking ('Hum!') is itself an assault.
a thing made for Alexander i.e. (a) as if he were a statue of Alexander the Great, or (b) sitting on a throne that might have been made for Alexander.
mercy i.e. he wants (lacks) mercy.
hale Haul.
inches Torture.
blown Wind-blown.
hautboys Oboes.
sackbuts Bass trumpets with trombone-like slides.
psalteries Harp-like stringed instruments.
Tabors Small side-drums.

Act V Scene 5

On their return to Rome, Volumnia, Virgilia and Valeria are greeted by the people.

Commentary

This is continued from Act V, Scene 4 by some editors, as there is no obvious change of location. However, the opening stage direction suggests processional movement, which is more effective if it fills a previously empty stage. The senator may then address the audience and his stage audience as if they are one. By his absence, and by the inevitable comparison with Act II, Scene 1, l.60, the scene dramatizes Coriolanus's isolation.

tribes i.e. plebeians; see III,3,11.
triumphant fires Bonfires.
Unshout i.e. cancel.
Repeal Recall, i.e. Coriolanus from banishment.

Act V Scene 6

In Corioles, Aufidius prepares to denounce Coriolanus to the lords of the city and the common people. Coriolanus returns from the campaign, claiming success and asserting his loyalty. Aufidius accuses him of treachery, and in the ensuing uproar Coriolanus is killed by conspirators.

Commentary

The victory celebration is succeeded by the menace and intrigue of this scene. Heroically unaware of any immediate danger, Coriolanus is once more (see Act III, Scene 3) defeated by conspiracy – on this occasion fed by the personal jealousy and hatred of Aufidius – in a political arena of easily manipulated emotions where violence predictably overcomes reason and justice. Aufidius is in the ascendancy and knows it; the outcome of his stage-management, the fall of a political innocent, is never in doubt. The despatch of accusatory letters initially damns Coriolanus, and manoeuvres him into a defensive position before he is aware of an attack. Aufidius is cautious enough to intend to 'proceed as we do find the people', but quickly assures himself and the consipirators of the necessary pretext. The veracity of 'I pawn'd/Mine honour to his truth' is stretched to: 'He water'd his new plots with dews of flattery', and Aufidius's history of the pride he took in doing himself wrong so incenses him, that he can scarcely tolerate the sycophantic interruption. Emphasizing

a notional Volscian possession of Rome, and only now inter-
preting the decision, in which he had acquiesced (V,3,194), as a
breaking of an oath of allegiance, and most of all by the belittling
references to Coriolanus's response to the deputation, Aufidius
carefully distorts the truth so that this charge of 'traitor' (see also
III,1,161) is almost impossible to answer. Rome was at Coriolanus's mercy, yet he made peace; he acted on his own
authority, without council of war; he listened to the pleading of
his family and was deeply moved. Coriolanus is defenceless
against calculated insinuation. Like other characters before him,
and for other reasons, Aufidius presents an image of Coriolanus
that suits his purpose. Populist diatribe overwhelms the pacific
cries of the judiciary. Coriolanus's uncharacterisitc proclamation
of his success suggests that the confident spectacle of his entry is
really an equivocating pretence. His predicament is the inevitable consequence of his humanity; the required self-justification
is uneasy. The word 'traitor' shatters the pose that necessity has
compelled him to adopt. Coriolanus is instantly the disdainful
soldier, and he is goaded by Aufidius's deriding of a sensibility
refined so painfully; he sweeps away all mean accusations in
defence of his honour, and recalls to the Volscians in Corioles
what has made him Coriolanus:

> 'Boy! False hound!
> If you have writ your annals true, 'tis there,
> That like an eagle in a dove-cote, I
> Flutter'd your Volscians in Corioles.
> Alone I did it. Boy!'

Coriolanus 'pulls all about his ears' (see III,2,1) and after an
almost ritual slaughter, the corpse is accorded an indignity that
ironically reverses Volumnia's prediction (I,3,46–7).

Refused a trial, and now that he is no longer a threat, Coriolanus is granted the proper formality of a 'noble memory'
among his enemy allies. The stage is emptied to the sound of a
dead march. Aufidius is a hollow man, who seems to regret what
he has done, even as he consolidates the power he has acquired
by doing it. Cruelty and malevolence appear to triumph, but the
audience's sympathies are with Coriolanus, who is renewed in
his fall.

city. There is some inconsistency here. The city is, for dramatic effect,
Corioles (lines 90 and 150) – despite 'native town', i.e. Antium (l.50).

purge Clear.

alms empoisoned i.e. destroyed by his own generosity.

wished us parties i.e. to be party to 'the same intent'.

deliver ... danger i.e. the conspirators will kill Coriolanus.

water'd ... flattery i.e. he corrupted Aufidius's followers by flattering them. There is no supporting evidence for this in the play or in the source.

stoutness Obstinacy.

files i.e. rank and file of troops.

wag'd ... countenance i.e. his smiles and favours were thought sufficient payment for Aufidius, as if the latter were a mercenary.

carried i.e. had Rome at his mercy.

my sinews ... him i.e. I will strain every nerve to defeat him.

women's rheum i.e. tears.

post Messenger.

along Stretched out.

After ... pronounc'd After his story is told in your manner.

found easy fines Suffered light punishment.

levies Troops raised.

answering ... charge Either (a) paying us only with expenses of the expedition (inconsistency l.77), or (b) justifying his action by the authority vested in him by us.

infected with Influenced (tainted) by.

counterpoise Outweigh.

drops of salt Tears.

whin'd and roar'd i.e. a reference to Coriolanus's evident distress, (V,3,182–90).

shall join i.e. the stripes (wounds) will join in rejecting the lie.

edges Swords.

judicious Judicial.

lawful i.e. in war.

owe Threaten.

one i.e. of the bearers.

Trail ... pikes At military funerals in Elizabethan England pikes were held in reverse.

memory Memorial, tomb.

Revision questions on Act V

1 What is the nature of the first two embassies to Coriolanus? What is their effect?

2 Analyse the argument/imagery/dramatic effect of Volumnia's speeches in V,3.

3 Compare Aufidius's account of the campaign (Act V, Scene 6) with that given by Coriolanus.

Shakespeare's art in *Coriolanus*
Introduction

Historical in subject matter, political in design, *Coriolanus* is the last of Shakespeare's tragedies. Shakespeare's primary intention is not historical verisimilitude, much less didactic political analysis and judgement, but the imaginative re-creation of a world of classical antiquity in which the central figure is a man of stature, whose tragic fall we partially understand, and wonder at:

> Whether 'twas pride,
> Which out of daily fortune ever taints
> The happy man; whether defect of judgement,
> To fail in the disposing of those chances
> Which he was lord of; or whether nature,
> Not to be other than one thing.

The tragedy derives from Coriolanus's hubristic pride, the accidents of circumstance, and the rigid nature of the soldier in a political world. The sense of loss and waste that the tragedy produces is also a cathartic reaffirmation of the ideals by which fallible mankind must live.

The stage history of the play has been chequered. Performances have ranged from the ridiculous (Nahum Tate's version (1681–2) including, among other effects, the torturing of young Martius, and the suicide of Virgilia when threatened with violation by Aufidius) to the partisan (a Comédie Française production of 1933–4 was received as fascist diatribe and provoked riots). The critical response to the text has been diverse: 'Shakespeare's most assured artistic success' (T. S. Eliot); 'tragical satire' (O. J. Campbell); 'grotesque tragedy' (K. Burke); 'the greatest of Shakespeare's comedies' (Bernard Shaw); 'rather a private and domestic than a public or historical tragedy' (Swinburne); 'a storehouse of political common-places' (Hazlitt); 'taking tragedy into an area of paradox beyond the effective reach of merely human pity' (Farnham). The reactions to the character of Coriolanus are equally varied: 'rather a schoolboy' (K. Muir); 'mechanical warrior' (Traversi); a slaying-machine' (G. W. Knight); 'an impossible person' (Bradley); 'splendid oaf' (J. Palmer); 'superb egoism ... the source of weakness and strength' (Dowden); 'his mother's puppet' (O. J. Campbell); 'his virtues stem from vicious pride' (Farnham); 'what has all along looked like pride in Coriolanus is but rebellion against standards and concessions that repel him' (Ellis- Fermor); 'hero-boy' (Brower).

Given the intimidating range of interpretation, eclecticism recommends itself. Its pervasive ambivalence – to the nature of Coriolanus the man and to that of Roman society – is, in its searching out of truth, the play's greatest strength.

The characters

Coriolanus

'To his surname Coriolanus longs more pride
Than pity'

The tragedy of Caius Martius Coriolanus is peculiarly his own.
No one else dies or is brought down through his actions; Rome,
with its factions, remains substantially the same: 'The noise that
banish'd Martius' is unshouted and the all-threatening fire
(V,1,14) becomes a triumphant image (V,5,3) in thanksgiving to
the gods for the life of the city; while in that other city, Corioles,
where Martius 'widow'd and unchilded many a one', the dead
march sounds. The dramatic paradox is typical of the prob-
lematic nature of the character and fall of Coriolanus. The play,
like the servingmen's vicarious enthusiasm for war, is 'sprightly
walking, audible and full of vent' and even when the protagonist
is not on the stage he remains the focus of interest, continuously
spoken of, if not always reliably.

Characters of major importance, for example Volumnia, Aufidius, Menenius, Brutus and Sicinius, judge him from personal
perspectives that the play forces us to question; and many
intricate passages of commentary are provided by peripheral
figures – citizens, soldiers, officers in the Capitol, spies, servants
to Aufidius, watchmen to Aufidius, conspirators. To misappro-
priate Menenius's allusion to Martius and Aufidius, Coriolanus
excites 'violent'st contrariety'; frequently described by his family
and patrician friends in superlative terms and regarded by the
people, the tribunes and his Volscian enemies with hostility,
resentment, suspicion and hatred. He is a man whose 'heart's his
mouth', and who is also curiously enigmatic.

It is not difficult to appreciate why literary critics have found
Coriolanus an unsympathetic character, and why perhaps *Coriolanus* has been with audiences the least popular of Shakespeare's
tragedies. Personally austere (II,2,5) and haughty, Coriolanus is
without any capacity for introspection. The rare soliloquies are
not explorations of mental process, they are simply statements of
condition (II,3,110; IV,4,12; V,3,20). Self-willed (II,2,136,145;
III,1,169), he is temperamentally volatile (III,1), seemingly con-

temptuous of humanity, and egotistically resentful (IV,5) of treatment he has partially provoked. Brought up (I,3,5–17) to believe in pure courage as earning love and conferring value, he is constantly presented as indifferent to life (V,3,35; V,4), as an inhuman puppet (V,4), a bloodletting automaton (II,2,107; I,3,34; I,5,19), a supra-human force (V,1,13) alternately godlike (II,1,217; III,1,80; IV,6,91) and bestial (IV,1,30; IV,7,34; V,6,114), consuming all before him in an ideal of valour that is self-sufficient beyond purpose, a pursuit of perfect death.

Coriolanus's public speech consists frequently of abrasive, ungenerous and unworthy invective (I,1 & 4; II,3; III,1). Apparently the antithesis of the Renaissance notion of the prince, he is unstatesmanlike (II and III) in the extreme, without any sense of community with those over whom he is set in authority. He seems to be incapable of conceiving of a balance of obligation between citizens and patricians. Far from concerning himself with the condition of the people (I,1) or acknowledging the justice of their complaint (III,1,118), Coriolanus rejects any acknowledgement of responsibility for 'fragments'. The nature of his authority would seem to be power without a sense of reciprocal obligation.

Yet this is also a man who is 'not/Of stronger earth than others', who cannot 'stand/As if a man were author of himself/And knew no other kin'. He was bred in the wars to which his mother sent him, became the consummate soldier of Cominius's high praise (II,2,81), a dutiful son (II,1,168; V,3), a tender and faithful husband (II,1,174; V,3,40), a proud father (V,3,70), an admired friend (II,1). He is deeply loved by all those who are good (I,3; II,1), and his qualities and service are praised by those whom they most intimidate (II,1,203; II,3,131; III,3,83; IV,5,102). Wholly unmercenary (I,1,41), preferring to serve the state as best he can in his own way (II,1,201) without expectation of reward (I,9,15), Coriolanus abhors flattery (I,9,44) and fears the corruption of pretence: 'Lest I surcease to honour mine own truth,/And by my body's action teach my mind/A most inherent baseness.' (III,2). Perceiving the appeasement of unrest as an erosion of political will, he urgently warns his 'good but most unwise' (III,1) equals that broad concessions of power, consequent on apprehension not preferential judgement, must threaten the integrity of the state; his vehemence is conviction and not thwarted ambition.

Ironically, however, the crucial test of Coriolanus's character comes in peacetime, through what is wanted for him (II,1,197) not by him. His failure is to suppose that he can avoid (II,2,136) the formalities he cannot in sincerity undertake, and, when persuaded, first by duty (II,2,133), and later by an appeal to necessity (III,2,26) and love (III,2,64), that he should debase himself, as he sees it, in the market place, to agree nominally (II,2,144; III,2,130) while in practice dissociating himself from his own performance (II,3,52; II,3,98 & 111; III,1) so that his latent fury at what he conceives of as a violation of established order, eventually erupts over a confused mob (II,3,70 & 111; III,1; III,3,68). The charade disintegrates because Coriolanus's instinct is for honour, not policy (III,2). He is unsuccessful at playing anyone other than the albeit imperfect man that he is. Coriolanus's tragic error is not his simmering resentment of a popular 'shall', or the periodic indiscipline of an ill-tempered 'Hang 'em!', but the agreement to 'frame his spirit' (III,2,97) to 'dissemble': '. . . must I/With my base tongue give to my noble heart/A lie that it must bear? Well I will do't'.

The tribunes are determined (III,3,1) to give a lesson to a muddled people who wish to acknowledge Coriolanus as consul (II,3,1–40) if he will let them (l.75), and he is too easily put 'to choler straight', precisely because his self-respect aborts the expedient falsehood of words to little purpose:

> . . . to speak
> To th'people; not by your own instruction . . .
> But with such words that are but roted in
> Your tongue, though but bastards and syllables
> Of no allowance to your bosom's truth. (III,2,52)

A further irony is that it was an accusation of pride (III,2,126) that finally swayed Coriolanus:

> Come all to ruin; let
> Thy mother rather feel thy pride than fear
> Thy dangerous stoutness . . . Do as thou list.
> Thy valiantness was mine, thou suck'st it from me,
> But owe thy pride thyself.

Here Volumnia makes what is for her at this point a rhetorically useful distinction between 'valour' ('the chiefest virtue' II,2,84) and a negative, self-centred aspect of pride, closer to arrogance and vanity than to a rigorous measurement of self against an inherited ideal (I,3). The distinction is made in the great intercession scene (V,3,170), on this occasion the inference being that self-absorbed pride is destructive of the peculiarly human impulse, compassion. The irony of this accusation, made by a mother who has 'bound' her son to her in the way Volumnia has (I,3,1–25 & 29–47) is compounded by its being an over-simplification and misreading of Coriolanus's character.

Instinct is obeyed (V,3,35), despite intention and expectation, and 'bond and privilege of nature' (V,3,25) do not break, although a promise must be kept (V,3,200; see also I,8,1). The final allegiance is to love, not to injured pride, to 'Great nature' and not to the false nobility of remembering wrongs (V,3,154) or the illusory discovery of a new 'constant' in betrayal (IV,4, 11; IV,5,66). (For recurring references to the idea of constancy, see: I,1,181 & 238; III,1,141; III,2,5; III,3,124; IV,1,51; V,2,91; V,3,20.)

Pride in its negative sense fails to corrupt Coriolanus, although the interpretation of the time would have it otherwise (I,1,31 & 257; II,1,229; II,3,151; III,1,54; III,2,129; V,3,171). It is true, though not in the sense meant by Volumnia (III,2,19), that Coriolanus might have been enough the man he was with striving less to be so; wrathful pride accelerates his fall and blinds him from understanding the folly of 'mere spite' (IV,5,83). Too absolute (III,2,39) a fidelity to his ideal, a nature 'too noble' and rigid (III,1,253) for the necessarily dynamic, mutable world, Coriolanus is himself an 'unnatural scene'. The tension between seeming and being, between what is said of Coriolanus and what he does, dramatizes the paradox that virtue carries with it the stamp of its own defect. Total dedication to heroic will is seen to be ultimately destructive of the community that such a will is created to defend. Volumnia fallaciously argues that the end (policy, the consulship) justifies the means (flattery, the sacrifice of honour); her education of Coriolanus has perfected the instrument of her ambition to a self-sufficiency that even she disowns (III,2,129). The courageous selflessness of thinking 'his country's dearer than himself (I,6,72) is a condition in which wrath will tend to overwhelm pity (I,9,84). The integral, indissoluble nature of character has spices of all qualities; Coriolanus is a divided being, just as Rome is a divided city.

Coriolanus never fully understands the folly of his renegade banishing of the world, but there is a redemptive element in his coming to realize a common humanity (V,3), come what may ('let it come'), in putting life before honour, in the final silence of a man of deeds submitting to a truth action cannot define; and in the sacrificial manner of his death, alone, in an enemy town. Trapped by words, surprise, conspiracy, and overwhelmed by numbers, in the greatness of his heart (V,6,103) he disdains untruth and death:

Cut me to pieces, Volsces, men and lads,
Stain all your edges on me. Boy! False hound!
If you have writ your annals true, 'tis there
That, like an eagle in a dove-cote, I
Flutter'd your Volscians in Corioles.
Alone I did it.

Coriolanus is goaded to heroic fury by the words 'traitor' and 'boy'; in this rage there is a suppressed acknowledgement of inadmissible imperfection. The 'constant', 'noble' warrior changed a mind (I,1,181) twice, and the fellow-feeling that eventually saves him from himself is 'unlike wrath', emotion accessible to reason, the realization that to be tender-minded does become a sword.

Volumnia

'There's no man in the world/more bound to's mother'
'the honoured mould/Wherein this trunk was framed'

Volumnia is a dignified patrician matron, scornful of 'woollen vassals' not of her 'ordinance' (social class) (III,2,9), intimidating those who oppose her (IV,2), contemptuous of weakness and fear, even in the face of death (V,3). Her love for Coriolanus and her pride in him have had a great part in making him what he is. She gave him 'valiantness' by her upbringing of him, and her description of this (I,3,1–25) is the first, powerful impression we get of this stern matriarch, who thanks the gods for the wounds that measure her son's achievements, and for whom heroic death has a beauty that defies life:

> ... The breast of Hecuba,
> When she did suckle Hector, look'd not lovelier
> Than Hector's forehead when it spit forth blood
> At Grecian sword contemning.

Her strength of character, manifest in her dominance of every scene in which she appears, is the source of Coriolanus's energy and courage, his personal pride, patrician sense of honour, love for family and friends, and his corrosive fury.

In Coriolanus's difference from his mother also lies the source of the drama and tragedy of his fall. Volumnia's pride in Coriolanus is partly ambition for him. Having lived to 'see inherited my very wishes' there is only one thing wanting, the consulship (II,1,196). To secure this she will have Coriolanus 'perform a part' (III,2,105) if necessary, just as she counsels a fine distinction between 'honour' and 'policy', which 'absolute' principle might not allow, but which expediency urges (see III,2 and compare with V,3). Volumnia persuades Coriolanus, against his hesitant sense of what is due to honour and to himself, to please her: 'I am in this/Your wife, your son, these Senators, the nobles;' and to flatter his way to power. Volumnia's encouragement of Coriolanus to 'dissemble with ... nature' (III,2,62) is largely responsible for the inevitable tragic consequences. On the first occasion Volumnia and Coriolanus are seen together, the son kneels to the mother in respect; and almost his first words to her are a warning of the impossibility of her dream: '... Know good mother/I had rather be their servant in my way/Than sway with them in theirs'.

Volumnia is a remorseless logician and tactician, and in both scenes of persuasion and intercession (III,2, and V,3) her deployment of reason and emotion ensures that the 'will' (III,2,136) and the 'dispatch' (V,3,180) that Coriolanus enacts are what she would have them. Volumnia uses the natural bond of affection as a means of attaining the end that is in her son's best interest, as she defines it.

Coriolanus obeys her demand that he should become consul, and having sworn revenge on the city that betrayed him, he obeys her demand that he break his promise to the Volsces. Volumnia wills victory at any cost. Coriolanus's victory is in refraining from it, and in knowingly compromising one allegiance so as to remain faithful to another. This is what Volumnia does not understand (V,3,185). In a special sense, then, Coriolanus does owe his pride to himself.

Volumnia never doubts the rightness of her conduct; there is no question of the sincerity of it. The peculiar dramatic strength of her appeal for mercy is in its fusion of pathos and conviction: '...Say my request's unjust/And spurn me back; but if it be not so,/Thou art not honest.' There is dramatic irony in Volumnia's return to Rome (V,5) just as her son returns alone to Corioles to die.

Menenius

'Old father Menenius'

Menenius is a patrician first and last, one 'o'th'right-hand file'. To say that he has always 'loved the people' is to pay tribute to the expansive temper of a 'humorous patrician ... one that converses more with the buttock of the night than with the forehead of the morning', rather than to describe his actual behaviour in the play. He satirizes the tribunes' conduct as 'herdsmen of the beastly plebeians', and explains away the people's grievances by means of a disingenuous fable (I,1,95). He condescends to his audience, diverting opposition by comic asides – and when the citizens are 'almost thoroughly persuaded' that opposition is futile and mistaken, that the patricians have truly cared for their 'masters ... friends ... neighbours' – Menenius turns to Martius to speak of the cowardice and lack of discretion of these 'rats' of Rome. The political skills, patrician sympathies, and predilection for compromise, amply demonstrated in the opening scene, are evident in his enthusiasm for Coriolanus's consulship (II,1 and II,2), his attempts to steer Coriolanus through the formalities of the appointment (II,2; III,2; III,3), his advice that Coriolanus should 'fit you to the custom' (II,2), and that public discourse should be conducted 'mildly' (III,1; III,2), in his admitting imperfections and absorbing criticism (III,1; III,3) and patching differences 'With cloth of any colour' (III,1). He wants to proceed by 'process' (III,1) when violence threatens, to retire unchallenging in 'peace' (IV,2) before the tribunes who have incited the mob to hoot Coriolanus out of Rome, and grows 'most kind' to them (IV,6) when he acknowledges that all is well and that it might have been better if Coriolanus 'could have temporiz'd' – although he can't resist the opportunity to taunt the 'good work' of Brutus and Sicinius and of their 'apron-men' when the city is threatened by Volscian attack. Menenius suits his conduct to his purpose, and to what the time will allow.

Garrulous, mocking, self-opinionated, patronizing and something of a trencherman, Menenius is also a warm-hearted, harmless old man, who desires nothing more than traditional advantage and conventional respect for his class, and deserved public honours for his friend. He sincerely loves his 'son' Coriolanus, and is loved in return. Menenius's jubilation at Coriolanus's victory is infectious, and his admiration and obvious pride in Coriolanus's battle scars is, in some ways, unaffectedly childlike. He is unaware of the effect on Coriolanus of the patrician pressure (indirect – love and expectation; direct – rhetoric) to dissemble, as Menenius understands neither the nature of the man nor the nature of society.

Menenius's approach to Coriolanus in the Volscian camp begins as a pathetic, absurd gesture, and ends in a dignified silence broken by the jeering sentries who are finally respectful of the spirited departure of a 'crack'd heart'. The redemption of Menenius from banality and buffoonery is to be found in his courage in defeat, and in his partial understanding that this 'dragon ... engine ... thing made for Alexander ... with no more mercy in him than there is milk in a male tiger' has been created by the unforgivable folly of Rome: 'The gods will not be good to us. When we banished him, we respected not them.' Menenius may not understand the organic theory of the state with which he fobs off the citizens' disgrace, but his perception of the culpability of the patricians implies a dawning awareness of collective responsibility.

Menenius provides an indirect commentary on the character of the hero. We partly interpret Coriolanus by the warmth of feeling he has for his old friend, and by the absence in Coriolanus of the physical and psychological self-indulgence, flattery, hypocrisy and political astuteness that characterize the cheerful master of convenience.

Brutus and Sicinius

'A brace of unmeriting, proud, violent, testy magistrates (alias fools)'

The tribunes are an indistinguishable pair of elderly, respectable (though not patrician) Romans, who are concerned with consolidating the power granted to them by the patricians. Envious and resentful of the arrogant authority of Martius (I,1,251), they are mean-spirited in their treatment of him (I,1,257 and III,3,140), and cynical in their political judgements (I,1,267 and II,3,232). They are cunning and devious in the exercise of their responsibilities as lawful guardians of the people's welfare. They 'suggest' (II,1,243) to the people Coriolanus's hatred of them, and 'that to's power he would/Have ... silenc'd their pleaders, and/Dispropertied their freedoms'. In the turbulent central section of the play, after the defeat of the Volsces, prior to the expulsion of Coriolanus from Rome, Brutus and Sicinius determine the action, 'lessoning' (schooling) their charges (II,3,175) to revoke (II,3,216) the election, efficiently marshalling the votes by 'tribes' (III,3,11) in order to do so. Coriolanus is not given a chance to answer (III,1,322), or repent (III,2,37) his words; he is deliberately manoeuvred (III,1,24 and III,3,25).

However, the tribunes' doubts about the intentions of Coriolanus and the possible effects of his consulship are not irrational in themselves, and they are fostered by Coriolanus's own reluctance to concede power to the people (II,2,146). The laconic observation of the 'pother' that the very presence of 'Coriolanus' inspires (II,1,203) is a recognition of the inherent instability and absurdity of popular acclaim as a measure of esteem: 'As if that whatsoever god that leads him/Were slily crept into his human powers,/And gave him graceful posture.' Therefore it may be well that their 'office may,/During his power, go sleep' and their reaction to this 'traitorous innovator' can be seen as a defence of the humanity of the citizens against the proud ruler who speaks of them as if he were 'a god to punish, not/A man of their infirmity'. Consensus politics does require a 'gentler spirit' (III,1,54), for 'What is the city but the people?' The innate, self-interested caution and the prudent moderation of Brutus and Sicinius cannot inspire admiration or affection, but neither is this necessarily as simple as unmitigated evil. The tribunes do seek to restore the people to their 'ancient strength' (IV,2,6) and having done so, Coriolanus's banishment is, albeit temporarily, a 'happier and more comely time' (IV,6), when, even Menenius, whom they had agreed to appoint 'the people's officer' (III,2,326) agrees that 'All's well, that might have been much better if/He could have temporiz'd'.

Menenius's speech at the beginning of Act II (Sc.1,45–95) is entertaining and persuasive: 'You know neither me, yourselves, nor any thing. You are ambitious for poor knaves' caps and legs. You wear out a good wholesome forenoon in hearing a cause between an orange-wife and a faucet-seller, and then rejourn the controversy of threepence to a second day of audience.'

(II,1,67–72) But even by this point we have learnt to regard Menenius as being not entirely reliable as a commentator, and his interpretation of the role of the tribunes does not allow for the fact that, disconcertingly, there is some truth in some of what the tribunes say, and justification for some of what they do. If this argument is accepted, it nevertheless constitutes a sharper criticism of them than is made by Menenius – who is not dissimilar to Brutus and Sicinius in having a desire to arrange events for the benefit of his own class, and who objects to the manner and results of the tribunes' action, rather than to their principles and motives.

Brutus and Sicinius deal in half-truths knowingly, and as such they are a more insidious force than Menenius – who is close to them – can recognize. The tribunes equate their political interest with the safety of the state, and Coriolanus equates the virtues of his class with the integrity of the state; neither is wholly correct, but we are made to see the honesty, at least, of Coriolanus's position by the duplicity of tribunes. They find politically unacceptable Coriolanus's expression of his reasons for doubting the wisdom of the movement towards democracy that the tribunes' appointment represents (III,1,118).

Brutus and Sicinius are hypocritical (II,3,260) and unprincipled in the charges they make against Coriolanus (III,3,63). They wield power without executive responsibility for its consequences. Populist demagogues, they throw into relief the self-effacing, disinterested aristocratic ideal, typified by Cominius.

Aufidius

'A lion that I am proud to hunt'

The martial virtues of Aufidius, presented as they are initially (I,1) serve to complement the personal heroism and military leadership of Coriolanus. Mutual respect is as much the keynote of early references as is competitive hatred. Aufidius admits to 'emulation', and Coriolanus to admiration: 'And were I anything but what I am,/I would wish me only he.' Each character finds his own qualities epitomized by the other. The intensity of this identification explains, ironically, the apparent inconsistency of Coriolanus in presenting himself, defenceless and exiled, to one he claims to hate 'Worse than a promise-breaker', and of Aufidius in giving an emotional welcome precisely according to the 'hospitable canon' that he had earlier vowed to defy:

>   ... know thou first,
> I loved the maid I married; never man
> Sigh'd truer breath; but that I see thee here,
> Thou noble thing, more dances my rapt heart
> Than when I first my wedded mistress saw
> Bestride my threshold.

The impulsive acceptance of the alien in these incongruously affectionate terms indicates the degree to which Aufidius (unconsciously at this point) covets the reputation of Coriolanus.

Aufidius feels himself to be diminished by the godlike stature of the man with whom he is inevitably compared, and with whom he compares himself. His 'valour's poison'd' by defeat, and later by the attempt to make Coriolanus 'more a friend than e'er an enemy'. Aufidius is doomed by his own jealousy and the rigidity of Coriolanus, and by the nature of the political realities, so caustically commented upon by the servants: 'Our general himself makes a mistress of him, sanctifies himself with's hand, and turns up the white o'th'eye to his discourse. But the bottom of the news is, our general is cut i'th'middle, and but one half of what he was yesterday.' The 'ancient envy' rankles, reduces Aufidius to the lies and innuendo of his seeking a pretext to strike, and to the taunting of Coriolanus with the new-found humanity that will cost him his life.

The treachery of a man whose nobility Coriolanus confessed to envying is a means of emphasizing the final redemption of the hero. Aufidius's lengthy assessment of Coriolanus's 'sovereignty of nature' (IV,7), subtly inserted before the final testing of the hero, is perceptive and relatively objective, and its conclusion is fatalistic: 'Our virtues/Lie in th'interpretation of the time'.

At the end of the play the implication is that, as the world judges, Aufidius might appear to be triumphant. Once a great soldier, Aufidius is, however, always the lesser man. He ends as a mean creature, who betrays and spitefully dishonours one who trusted him, a 'measureless liar' who lacks Coriolanus's heart. The martial virtues that have characterized both men are seen to be in themselves an inadequate foundation for society; when such values are paramount, in the service of nothing but themselves, they corrupt the individual – and the life of the community, for whose benefit they are nurtured, becomes prey to its own creation: 'One fire drives out one fire, one nail one nail;/ Rights by rights falter; strengths by strengths do fail'.

Virgilia

'My gracious silence'

A deceptively significant character, Virgilia appears in relatively few scenes in this long play, and has little discernible influence in the action. Reticent by nature, she is seen more than she is heard, and when she speaks it is often to invoke the blessings of the gods on her husband. Volumnia chides her for her concern when Martius is absent in the wars: for her refusal to be seen in public until he returns; for her apprehension at the possibility that he has been wounded; and for her speechless weeping before the stern oppressor (V,3). This acute sensitivity should not be taken for weakness. Virgilia has the strength of character to pursue her own course, and to think and feel as she does, despite the blandishments of the authoritative Volumnia; this is perfectly apparent in the first scene in which she appears. She joins her mother-in-law in roundly condemning the tribunes for hounding Coriolanus out of Rome, and when Volumnia threatens Coriolanus that if he attacks Rome she will die by her own hand, Virgilia's determination is expressed in terms that remind her husband of his self-destructive denial of 'All bond and privilege of nature' – and if he is willing to tread even on the mother who bore him, then he must also defile the wife 'That brought you forth this boy to keep your name/Living to time'.

Virgilia's silence and depth of feeling give her a grace and nobility that Volumnia, with all her rhetoric and authority, cannot equal. Virgilia never attempts to persuade her husband to be anything other than his natural self – natural as defined by the ideas her presence implies: love, loyalty, selflessness, tenderness. She is an 'aspect of intercession' that, by the purity of her affection, overcomes the resolution of Coriolanus. The tension of the play's moments of stillness owes a great deal to the sensibility that Virgilia's presence evokes. When Martius returns as 'Coriolanus', it is Virgilia's reception of him that is the most moving, and the only one that can move him to reveal something of an inner self that feels more than he might himself suppose for those whose suffering allows his victory.

> My gracious silence, hail!
> Would'st thou have laughed and I come coffin'd home
> That weep'st to see triumph? Ah, my dear,
> Such eyes the widows in Corioles wear,
> And mothers that lack sons.

This scene (II,1) prepares us for the later one (V,3) in which Virgilia is 'the best' of Coriolanus, whose eyes 'melt' his tyranny by reminding him of allegiances greater than 'honour'. These great moments of feeling are the consequence of the juxtaposition of her character with circumstances that are conditioned by the antithesis of what she is. Therefore Virgilia is important for the effects generated by her presence rather than for what she says or does merely. She represents an order, and a reverence for life that stands apart from and superior to a sense of imminent darkness and strife that would otherwise dominate the play to the exclusion of love and hope.

Setting, structure and themes

Setting

The Rome of *Coriolanus* is a small city-state on the Tiber: a fledgling republic, industrious and warlike, threatening and being threatened by its neighbour states. Roman offices (consuls, tribunes, senators, aediles, lictors), classical allusions (e.g. Jupiter, Juno, Mars, Triton, Hydra, Hector, Hecuba) and references to the buildings and features of the town (Capitol, market-place, walls, gates, Tarpeian rock, Tiber) contribute in atmosphere and detail, and by their suggestion of rigidity, to a sense of tension in a confined world, where power-play between interdependent factions (patricians and plebeians) threatens disintegration of the state.

The vitality of the setting is Elizabethan. The insurrection (I,1) reflects English disturbances of 1607 rioting in Leicestershire, Northamptonshire and Warwickshire in protest at enclosure of common land, and perhaps that of 1597 in Oxfordshire. And, of course, the linguistic detail is Elizabethan.

The local colour of all Shakespeare's plays is that of Elizabethan England, whether the story is one of Rome, Egypt or Denmark, and in whatever age. Nowadays we should demand strict accuracy in scenery, costume and topical references, but then, for playwright and audience alike, the life and spirit of a play mattered more than strict accuracy in local colour. 'It is the spirit which giveth life.' People saw in the drama a reflection of their own life and experience; its appeal was in no wise analytical or educational, but human.

Further, in those days people were relatively untravelled and few were formally educated and would not pounce on anachronisms.

It must be remembered that there was no scenery and no period costume. Incongruities which become apparent beside 'realistic' scenery would not be noticed then. In references to a character's dress it would be farcical, were the references historically correct but also, for example, to something the character was not actually wearing on the stage.

Coriolanus takes place nominally in Rome, Corioles and

Antium, in 492 BC, but we are really never very far from the England Shakespeare knew. Rome has its 'charter' like any important English borough of the reign of Elizabeth I. Trouble-makers in 'stinking greasy caps' roam the streets 'with bats and clubs'. Coriolanus finds looters packing up 'cushions, leaden spoons, irons of a doit, doublets'. As he walks in procession:

> stalls, bulks, windows,
> Are smother'd up, leads fill'd, and ridges hors'd
> With variable complexions, all agreeing
> In earnestness to see him . . .
> . . . Matrons flung gloves,
> Ladies and maids their scarfs and handkerchers,
> Upon him as he pass'd.

Soldiers are armed with 'steel pikes' and 'corslets' and use battering rams. Workmen with thoroughly Elizabethan names ('Hob and Dick') are distinguished from the upper classes by their rough-spun woollen garments ('woollen vassals'); 'kitchen malkins' wear 'lockram'. We hear of an 'orange-wife' and a 'faucet-seller', and drachmas, doits, groats and pence are all current coin of the realm. People play bowls, enjoy coursing ('like a fawning greyhound in the leash, to let him slip at will'), listen to ballad-makers, and are punished by being put 'i'the stocks'. Volumnia invokes 'the red pestilence' on the Roman 'trades'. People in spectacles walk the Roman streets.

Coal is three times mentioned; 'the coal of fire upon the ice' would bring to the memory of the audience the contemporary winter of 1608, when the Thames froze in London in January and fires were lit upon the ice. The musical instruments are hautboys, drums, 'trumpets, sackbuts, psalteries and fifes, tabors and cymbals', not all English, it is true, but names familiar to English audiences through the Bible. The theology is a composite one made up of 'augurers' and 'flamens', 'divines', 'graves i' the holy churchyard', 'under fiends', 'hell' and 'fires of heaven', and it is customary to 'grace 'fore meat'. When Aufidius took his 'wedded mistress' home, his heart danced to see her 'bestride his threshold', not a Roman ceremony.

The world of the play is both period and contemporary, and is, therefore, timeless in its imitation of human nature and condition, by the creation of character and relationships and the momentum of public events. The Roman setting (with its Elizabethan resonance) provides a narrative and themes that are of use to the dramatist, but it does not determine or confine the meaning of the play.

Structure

One of Shakespeare's longest plays, *Coriolanus* is marvellously taut and economical in its organization, a single plot, symmetrical in pattern. It is a series of conflicts, variously and contentiously interpreted by the play's multiple commentators: Rome and its enemy town Antium; Coriolanus and his rival Aufidius; the patricians and Coriolanus versus the tribunes and the plebeians; Coriolanus the son versus Volumnia the mother; Coriolanus's 'natural' inner self versus his fatal pride. The play simultaneously dramatizes instability in the public life of the city and in the private life of Coriolanus; the action moves from this turbulence to the silence of Coriolanus, holding Volumnia's hand; and to the last scene of dishonour and triumph.

Disregarding the act divisions, the structure of the play may be considered as follows: the introductory scenes (I,1,2,3) of civil strife, enemy action and domestic anxiety lead to the first movement – the war between the Romans and the Volsces, culminating in the taking of Corioles. The second movement is that of the major central scenes (II,1–2; IV,2) in Rome where Coriolanus is at different times and several ways in opposition to the citizens, the patricians, Volumnia, and the tribunes. The final movement, prefaced by the interlude of the spies (IV,3) includes Coriolanus's arrival in Antium (IV,4) to join Aufidius, the intercession scenes, and the death of Coriolanus.

Parallels and reversals within this pattern create the ironic counterpoint necessary to the essentially equivocal nature of the play – reality is always belied by appearances. The nature of the state and the nature of Coriolanus are continuously examined. Rome is a city that has elevated 'virtus' to the point of the denial of 'pietas', where the energies of love are sublimated to the destructive urge, where the spilling of life-blood, to Volumnia at least, carries a ritual, religious significance, where wounds must be shown in market-place, where words to little purpose are the medium of exchange – a city that lives by the heroic valour that almost destroys it. The 'Alone'-ness of Coriolanus is his strength and his weakness. He leads the citizen-soldiers to victory, deserting and being deserted by them in time of peace. He is intemperately modest, expecting the rewards he has earned and omitting the expression of gratitude to those who made victory possible and whose prerogative it is to give; he slights the praise of what he has achieved by referring to what he might have done; admiring and hating Aufidius, Coriolanus turns to him when outcast from Rome, and is eventually betrayed by him. Coriolanus is also the man whose death saves the city, who is freed from self-tyranny by his submission to the feelings evoked by the presence of his mother, wife and child, who does truly owe his pride himself because of his fidelity to a notion of 'honour' that he alone understands (III,2). All the play's triumphs foreshadow misfortune: the victor of Corioles is banished; the tribunes are terrified by the force they have unleashed; Volumnia returns to Rome a goddess, as Aufidius treads on her son's corpse.

Themes

The principal ideas recurrent in *Coriolanus* are considerations of ideals upon which a society can be securely based; the need for harmony within the individual; and the central importance of acknowledged interdependence to the integrity of a society.

The survival of any state at some time demands a patriotism that will sacrifice self. The play suggests that, in its extremest form, martial valour (as Volumnia thinks of it) is ultimately destructive of the humanity of the individual and subsequently of the community of which he is a part. The education of Coriolanus has been an infusion of 'valiantness' (III,2,128) from a mother (see I,3,5–25) whose precepts (IV,1,9–11) have made him invincible, and a training in 'a cruel war'. Cominius's conditional 'if it be' (II,2,85) is rhetorical: 'valour is the chiefest virtue' (l.84) in patrician Rome.

The virtus (see the first extract from North's Plutarch, printed in *Source* pp.13–15) that protects the city against the periodic depredations of the Volsces, and which enables the city to grow by conquest, is of necessity inflexible. In 'honour' (III,2,41 & 121) Coriolanus disdains the petty compromise of 'policy', exiles himself from the world (IV,4,23–4) and becomes a 'lonely dragon', spoiling what he should protect. Pietas – the loving respect owed to family, country and gods – overcomes virtus (V,3); the hero sacrifices himself so that the society may continue to exist. By implication, therefore, love, fidelity and friendship have a meaning and sufficiency that heroic, martial courage cannot itself aspire to, since it is a destructive force from which alone order cannot be derived. Essentially its virtue is acquired through the defence of other virtues.

In the character of Coriolanus and the relationship between himself and Volumnia we see in individual terms a dramatization of the values and forces that constitute the organic life of the state. If a man is to be whole, his inner harmony derives from 'Great nature' (V,3), not second nature (IV,1,9–11), and the context of his nobility is the wholesomeness – that is, justice – of the society he serves.

The special political quality of *Coriolanus* is its creation of live political feeling and process: the circularity of imbalance; agitation; response; debate; interpretation; machination; opposition; compromise; and the uncertainty of resolution – a mutable world of jostling individuals and their uneasy dependence on the curtailment that constitutes government. The play is concerned with practical problems of order: class conflict; private virtue versus public good; the subsuming of the vital, responsible individual citizen by the anonymous and volatile crowd; the obstruction of the egalitarian ideal by inherited or institutional inequalities; the metamorphosis of rational advantage into opportunism; threats from external enemies and internal factions; the appetite for power and the need for its restraint; the tension that occurs during the modification of any dynamic system of government; the inevitable imperfection of the ruler and irresponsibility of the ruled; the education of authority.

The purpose of the artistic imitation of all of these phenomena is exploration, not judgement; and the several 'fragments' of the whole are given 'voices' that must be variously interpreted. Patricians can be magnanimous and mean; plebeians are kindly and vicious. Selfish groups and egotistic individuals will always pose a threat to the unity of a state.

The fable of the belly (I,1,95) provides the play's metaphor for the organic theory of social relationships, and Shakespeare's literary sources express a universal analogy. The state is an ordered whole (secular in *Coriolanus*, though the audience would recall the theological parallel from I Corinthians, 12) and this is the answer to conflicting power claims, to demands for equality or for a shift in the balance of social roles. Menenius's speech, however, is inseparable in argument from his manner of making it, and from the language of its expression. It conveys the unhealthy condition of the body politic. His political sedative is tactless, offered to the citizens who are hungry in time of super-fluity. It is the stomach that rules, smiling as it does so, and not 'the kingly crown'd head'. Questioning of the absolute character of the assertion that, 'No public benefit which you receive/But it proceeds or comes from them to you,/And no way from your-selves' is evaded with thinly disguised invective. Bread alone (Deuteronomy, 8,3; St Matthew, 4,4) is seen to be insufficient reason for men to live together. The palpable insincerity of Menenius's use of the argument presents it in a pejorative light. *Coriolanus* counters the over simplification of the analogy.

Style

Almost one quarter of the play is in *prose*, a remarkably high proportion for Shakespeare's tragedies and last plays, allowing flexibility in range of expression and variety of dramatic effect. The important and noble characters, who normally speak in verse, speak in prose in their less intense moments (the ladies for much of Act I, Scene 3, and Coriolanus at some time in Act I, Scene 1, and Act IV, Scene 5). Citizens and functionaries lower in the social scale for the most part speak in prose, except when they attempt to express elevated ideas (I,1; II,2,1–35; II,3; IV,3). Comic scenes of commentary are presented in colloquial prose (IV,5, especially 149–240, and the watchmen in V,2).

The basis of Shakespeare's *verse* is iambic pentameter. The syllabic stress generally follows the accents of normal speech, and modifications to the dominant pattern contribute to the cumulative rhythmical effect, as do other devices such as syntactical inversion, enjambement, caesura, elision. Shakespeare's vocabulary is extraordinarily rich and subtle. Words are often applied unusually (virgin'd, godded, lurch'd) or repeated so that additional meaning, sometimes dramatic irony, is acquired by the audience's retrospective consideration of context. A similar effect, one of thematic reverberation, is achieved by the recurrence of significant words like 'pride', 'constant', 'power', 'service', and most particularly of the names, each of which is partial, by which Martius is identified: 'Coriolanus', 'god', 'traitor', 'boy'.

The *imagery* of the play is intricately patterned. Menenius's fable of the belly introduces the idea of the state as a body, and references to the state of health of its 'members' (lungs, head, eye, heart, leg, brain, nerves, veins, toe), which ('digest things rightly', 'itch', 'scabs', 'musty superfluity') and destruction ('canker'd', 'tearing/His country's bowels out') are then continuous. The State is Hydra-headed, leaderless, and Coriolanus, an engine of death, is an actor who is prompted to a part he cannot play until, by slippery turns, he descends to 'th'city of kites and crows'. Animal images abound, to the detriment of all, conveying a sense of humanity preying upon itself: citizens are rats, curs, geese, wolves, crows, minnows. Coriolanus is alternately a dog, wolf, serpent, grub, or a lion, osprey, eagle, dragon. The fire images in the scenes of Coriolanus's revenge (V,1,14 & 64; V,2,7 & 70; V,3,181) suggest the imminence of a consuming purification.

The play's *tone* is powerful, discordant, clamorous, harsh (see descriptions of Coriolanus, II,2,107; V,4,18). In a play of public debate and private silence, an objective public theatre, there is a language of expression and not introspection, a notable absence of the reflective and the lyrical. Even the humour has a cutting edge: Menenius and the citizens heckling one another (I,1), Menenius and the tribunes exchanging insults (II,1), the citizens good-naturedly laughing at their own inconsistencies (II,3,17–35), Aufidius's servingmen (IV,5) marvelling at the ironies of life, and the Volscian watchmen deflating Menenius (V,2). Characters have their especial voices; and as Coriolanus, of whom all tongues speak, has about one quarter of the play's lines, his tirades and the rhetorical energy of his argument typify what is gaunt and compelling about the style of *Coriolanus*.

General questions

1 Discuss Volumnia's role in Coriolanus.

Guideline notes for an answer

Consider her upbringing of her son – I,3 – and its effect, e.g.
as described by Cominius in II,2; her ambition for him; her
fierce maternal love that she nevertheless subordinates to her
patriotism; her belief in 'valiantness', and what this means in
the thematic scheme of the play.

Show how her persuasion of Coriolanus – III,2 and V,3 –
dramatizes their differences more than their similarities, e.g.
in the 'honour' versus 'policy' argument, and in the relative
silence of Coriolanus. Examine the ironies implicit in her role;
through the power of her love she moves Coriolanus to act a
part and to debase himself, her willingness to dissemble gives
a different perspective from which we judge the 'pride' of
Coriolanus; she returns to Rome a patroness while Aufidius
treads on Coriolanus's neck.

'There's no man in the world/More bound to's mother'? In
what respects is this true, and in what respects is it an inadequate definition of the character of Coriolanus?

2 How far do you agree that Coriolanus is noble and virtuous
but far from wise?

3 Discuss the condition of Rome in *Coriolanus*.

4 In what ways can *Coriolanus* be said to be a political play with
contemporary relevance?

5 How do you account for the fact that *Coriolanus* has not been
one of Shakespeare's most popular plays?

6 How far is the fall of Coriolanus attributable to his pride?

7 How important in the play is what other characters say about
Coriolanus?

8 Discuss Shakespeare's debt to North's *Plutarch*.

9 Which do you think is the play's most powerful scene? Carefully justify your view.

10 Examine the role of the crowd of citizens in *Coriolanus*.

11 Discuss the conflict between honour and policy in *Coriolanus*.

12 What is the importance, in the play as a whole, of Menenius's fable of the belly?

13 Consider the effect of the structural parallels and reversals in *Coriolanus*.

14 Do you agree that Coriolanus is 'an impossible person'? (Bradley)

15 How does *Coriolanus* illustrate the 'wonderful philosophic impartiality' (Coleridge) of Shakespeare's politics?

16 How far do you agree with the view that in the last scene of the play 'the tragic feelings of pity and fear have little place'? (Bradley)

17 Do you agree that there is a satirical and even a humorous element in *Coriolanus*?

18 Show how *Coriolanus* is a noisy, public play.

19 Do you agree that in *Coriolanus* the characters use language and imagery appropriate to them?

20 How far do you agree that the play lacks imaginative depth and tragic atmosphere?

21 What is meant by the statement that 'pride is the essence of Martius's nature, at once his vice and his virtue'?

22 Show how, although a long play, *Coriolanus* is carefully structured.

23 Do you find it possible to sympathize with Coriolanus?

Further reading

There is a wealth of literature available. The student will find the following a useful and rewarding selection:

The introductions to these editions of *Coriolanus*:

The Arden Shakespeare, edited by Philip Brockbank, published by Methuen, 1976.

The New Swan Shakespeare, edited by John Ingledew, published by Longman, 1975.

The New Penguin Shakespeare, edited by G. R. Hibbard, published by Penguin Books, 1967.

Coriolanus in the 'Casebook' series, edited by B. A. Brockman, published by Macmillan, 1977.

'Studies in English Literature': Coriolanus by Brian Vickers, published by Edward Arnold, 1976.

Pan study aids Titles published in the Brodie's Notes series

W. H. Auden Selected Poetry

Jane Austen Emma Mansfield Park Northanger Abbey
Persuasion Pride and Prejudice

Anthologies of Poetry The Poet's Tale The Metaphysical Poets

Samuel Beckett Waiting for Godot

Arnold Bennet The Old Wives' Tale

William Blake Songs of Innocence and Experience

Robert Bolt A Man for All Seasons

Harold Brighouse Hobson's Choice

Charlotte Brontë Jane Eyre

Emily Brontë Wuthering Heights

Geoffrey Chaucer (parallel texts editions) The Franklin's Tale
The Knight's Tale The Miller's Tale The Nun's Priest's Tale
The Pardoner's Tale Prologue to the Canterbury Tales
The Wife of Bath's Tale

John Clare Selected Poetry and Prose

Wilkie Collins The Woman in White

Joseph Conrad Heart of Darkness The Nigger of the
Narcissus & Youth

Daniel Defoe Journal of a Plague Year

Charles Dickens David Copperfield Dombey and Son Great
Expectations Hard Times Little Dorrit Oliver Twist
Our Mutual Friend

Gerald Durrell My Family and Other Animals

George Eliot Middlemarch The Mill on the Floss Silas Marner

T. S. Eliot Murder in the Cathedral Selected Poems

J. G. Farrell The Siege of Krishnapur

William Faulkner As I Lay Dying

Henry Fielding Joseph Andrews

F. Scott Fitzgerald The Great Gatsby

E. M. Forster Howards End A Passage to India

E. Gaskell North and South

William Golding Lord of the Flies The Spire

Oliver Goldsmith Two Plays of Goldsmith: She Stoops to
Conquer The Good Natured Man

Graham Greene Brighton Rock The Human Factor The Power
and the Glory The Quiet American

Thomas Hardy Chosen Poems of Thomas Hardy
Far from the Madding Crowd The Mayor of Casterbridge
Return of the Native Tess of the d'Urbervilles
The Trumpet Major The Woodlanders

L. P. Hartley The Go-Between The Shrimp and the Anemone

Joseph Heller Catch-22

Ernest Hemingway A Farewell to Arms

Barry Hines Kes

Aldous Huxley Brave New World

Henry James Washington Square

Ben Jonson Volpone

James Joyce A Portrait of the Artist as a Young Man Dubliners

John Keats Selected Poems and Letters of John Keats

Ken Kessey One Flew over the Cuckoo's Nest

D. H. Lawrence The Rainbow Selected Tales Sons and Lovers

Harper Lee To Kill a Mockingbird

Laurie Lee Cider with Rosie

Thomas Mann Death in Venice & Tonio Kröger

Christopher Marlowe Doctor Faustus Edward the Second

W. Somerset Maugham Of Human Bondage

Gavin Maxwell Ring of Bright Water

Arthur Miller The Crucible Death of a Salesman

John Milton A Choice of Milton's Verse Comus and Samson
Agonistes Paradise Lost I, II

Sean O'Casey Juno and the Paycock The Shadow of a
Gunman and the Plough and the Stars

George Orwell Animal Farm 1984

John Osborne Luther

Alexander Pope Selected Poetry

J. D. Salinger The Catcher in the Rye

Peter Shaffer The Royal Hunt of the Sun

William Shakespeare Antony and Ceopatra As You Like It
Coriolanus Hamlet Henry IV (Part I) Henry IV (Part II)
Henry V Julius Caesar King Lear Love's Labour's Lost Macbeth
Measure for Measure The Merchant of Venice A Midsummer
Night's Dream Much Ado about Nothing Othello Richard II
Richard III Romeo and Juliet The Sonnets The Taming of the
Shrew The Tempest Twelfth Night The Winter's Tale

G. B. Shaw Pygmalion Saint Joan

Richard Sheridan Plays of Sheridan: The Rivals; The Critic;
The School for Scandal

John Steinbeck The Grapes of Wrath Of Mice and Men &
The Pearl

Tom Stoppard Rosencrantz and Guildenstern are Dead

J. M. Synge The Playboy of the Western World

Dylan Thomas Under Milk Wood

Flora Thompson Lark Rise to Candleford

Anthony Trollope Barchester Towers

Mark Twain Huckleberry Finn

Keith Waterhouse Billy Liar

Evelyn Waugh Decline and Fall Scoop

John Webster The White Devil

H. G. Wells The History of Mr Polly The War of the Worlds

Oscar Wilde The Importance of Being Earnest

William Wordsworth The Prelude (Books 1, 2)

William Wycherley The Country Wife

W. B. Yeats Selected Poetry